LOCATION SCOUTING AND MANAGEMENT HANDBOOK

LOCATION SCOUTING AND MANAGEMENT HANDBOOK

Television • Film • Still Photography

Robert G. Maier

Focal Press
Boston • London

Focal Press is an imprint of Butterworth–Heinemann.

Copyright © 1994 by Butterworth–Heinemann.
Ɽ   A member of the Reed Elsevier group.
All rights reserved.

Recognizing the importance of preserving what has been written, it is the ∞ policy of Butterworth–Heinemann to have the books it publishes printed on acid-free paper, and we exert our best efforts to that end.

PHOTOGRAPHS: Robert Maier, unless otherwise noted.

Library of Congress Cataloging-in-Publication Data

Maier, Robert G.
  Location scouting and management handbook : television, film and still photography / by Robert G. Maier.
    p.   cm.
  Includes index.
  ISBN 0-240-80152-0 (acid-free paper)
  1. Motion picture locations. 2. Television program locations.
  I. Title.
PN1995.67.A1M35   1994   94-13461
791.43'023 -- dc20   CIP

British Library Cataloguing-in-Publication Data

A catalogue record for this book is available from the British Library.

Butterworth–Heinemann
313 Washington Street
Newton, MA 02158

10 9 8 7 6 5 4 3 2
Printed in the United States of America

This book is dedicated to Catheryn Ann Casey Maier whose marvelous patience enabled her family to put up with a life in the production department.

Contents

Preface

Location scouting and management has its difficult moments and aspects, but for people-oriented and organizational-minded souls who possess a definite creative flair, the job can be very rewarding. For those who enjoy it and work hard at it, location scouting and management will lead to the higher levels of production administration and management.

Both people working within the industry and people looking to break into it express a lot of interest in the nuts-and-bolts techniques of location scouting and management. Such work requires an interesting mix of real-world "savvy" and a knowledge of the particular requirements of media production. The use of locations in production has increased at an incredible rate in recent years. Today, a wide range of productions—including feature films, TV commercials, music videos, industrial and educational films, TV movies and series, PBS documentaries, still photography, and reality-based TV docudramas—use locations instead of studios out of choice, not financial necessity.

Location scouting involves finding the *best* location, *all things considered*—and there is a lot to consider. It is a process of elimination as the scout discovers new things about each location possibility that make it either more or less suitable for a shoot. Location management involves maintaining a location as the production company prepares to use it and during the shoot so that everything goes as smoothly as possible.

Location Scouting and Management Handbook provides an in-depth but easily understandable examination of the work of the location scout and manager. It surveys proper techniques, means, tools, and procedures that will enable even production novices to understand and begin to undertake professional-level location work.

The book starts with a brief history of location shooting and then traces the process of location scouting and management from the beginning to the end of a production. Although various types of productions are covered, the primary focus is on motion picture productions, simply because their complexity creates greater demands. However, much of what is discussed applies to everything from a student video to a high-fashion photography session.

Each chapter addresses a major issue in location scouting and management, generally in the sequence in which that issue arises during a production. As questions about a particular location are answered, more is learned about its suitability as a candidate for the best location, and the location person can then take the next step toward including or excluding that location as a good possibility.

This is a guidebook that takes the reader from A to Z and will, by the end, have provided an overview of what it takes to scout. Along the way, it offers advice and hints, but it is not an instruction manual. Media production is not mass production. Every photograph, every TV show, and every movie is different. Each involves different people, different scenes, different stories. Therefore, this book cannot possibly describe all the situations that location people will face. It can only offer guideposts to help them navigate the never-before-charted demands of each unique production. Although it can be a confusing, frustrating route, it also can be exhilarating. Hopefully, this book will make the journey a little less painful.

Robert G. Maier
Davidson, NC

www.rgmaier@mindspring.com

Acknowledgments

I wish to thank Kenny Klompus and Allan Charles, of Charles Street Films in Baltimore, for their help with the TV commercial script and storyboard; Steve Apicella for the use of his home, where most of this book was written; Lynn and Lars Balck for their patient technical assistance; David Wilgus for his drawing in Chapter 3; Carole Patterson and Cohen Insurance in New York for their assistance with insurance questions; Chris Carroll and Kathleen Stapleton of Carolina Production Services, Charlotte, for the use of their Arri 35BL camera; Leo Eaton for my introduction to international production; Jane Began of Maryland Public Television for her support; Robert Mugge for taking me to the most exotic locations; Dr. Luc Cuyvers for his expertise with European culture; Robert Goald who suggested I call Focal Press with the idea to do this book; and my parents who encouraged and taught me to write.

I also wish to thank the residents and businesses of Davidson, North Carolina, whose homes and properties appear in these pages.

1

Why Location, Location, Location?

THE EARLY DAYS

One of the most charming stories told about the very early days of cinema describes the primitive short movie of a horse-drawn fire engine careening down a city street toward the camera. Audiences watched enthralled as the flickering black-and-white images on the wall created a shadowy, virtual reality. It also scattered them in panic when it seemed that the gigantic horses and monstrous fire engine would surely burst into the room and crush them all. Chairs and benches went flying as audience members scrambled away in terror. Of course, they felt silly when the lights came up, but the stunning power of these "real" things, places, and events was not lost on pioneering filmmakers. They discovered that true-to-life situations shot in actual locales had an undeniable impact on audiences.

Particularly in the United States, filmmakers from the very beginning sought to broaden the scope of their productions by taking them outside of the often artificial confines of the set and the stage. Silent filmmakers loved to shoot on location. Their most daring stunts were performed outdoors—on ice-filled rivers, hanging from the sides of buildings, swinging from the struts of a biplane, or on the cowcatchers of speeding steam locomotives. If it moved, they wanted to shoot it.

The most expansive and financially successful epics from the earliest days through the late 1920s, such as *Birth of a Nation* and *The General*, included much location shooting. In fact, most silent films required a great deal of location work. For three decades, the earliest filmmakers combed forests, fields, and neighborhoods to give their films an extra special look that audiences wanted, at a price they could afford.

Furthermore, the first cameras were hand-cranked and rather small, simple machines. They were easy to carry, put on a car, or even take up in the earliest airplanes. The first film stocks were nowhere near as sensitive as today's and required lots of light. The outdoors offered plenty of light, and it was free. There were other benefits as well. Shooting on location was cheaper because it enabled production companies to avoid leasing a shooting stage, building sets, procuring decorations, or using expensive, bulky, lighting equipment. On location, producers received a great deal of production value at very little cost.

To procure all these benefits, producers needed a sharp person who could go out and find the right locations— locations that satisfied the script requirements and perhaps added some visual interest or even grandeur but would not be too difficult to get to or break the budget. And thus was created the job of the location scout.

THE ADVENT OF SOUND

The rapid emergence of synchronized, recorded sound in the late 1920s immediately drove the vast majority of productions inside Hollywood's hastily built sound stages. Sensitive microphones coupled to complex recording devices and behemoth, soundproof cameras weighing well over 200 pounds made it impractical, if not impossible, to take a production outside. For the most part, the excitement of dynamic location shooting went the way of the handsome but squeaky-voiced leading man.

In its place came the tightly choreographed singing and dancing spectacles of Busby Berkeley and the stagy dramas in which nothing was real, and even shots of the countryside were just fuzzy rear projections captured by a second-rate second-unit photographer. The sound stage's doors were locked, and filmmakers became virtual prisoners of the microphone and of the factory mentality of Hollywood's studio moguls, who were just as happy to keep the productions under their constant vigil anyway. It was an era of constriction and artificiality in American cinema, and it lasted for three decades.

The smaller European film industries could not so easily afford sprawling Hollywood-type sound stage complexes, so they approached the sound era a bit differently. Instead of trying to create an expensive, perfect sound-recording environment, European producers continued to shoot their films on appropriate locations and just postdubbed the sound in a studio, with the actors lip-synching their dialogue. European directors also relied much more on purely visual storytelling, using considerably less dialogue than their American counterparts, who flaunted the technology of their "all-talking, all-singing" pictures.

THE RETURN TO LOCATION SHOOTING

In the early 1960s, a filmmaking revolution was spurred with the development of several extraordinary pieces of film production equipment that are still widely used today—namely, the new generation of handheld 35mm motion picture cameras and the Swiss-made Nagra sound recorder. Each of these new types of equipment was nearly *ten* times smaller and lighter than the equivalent equipment being used in Hollywood. They were designed to take advantage of the latest electromechani-

Figure 1.1 Arriflex 35BL III handheld 35mm motion picture camera. Earlier versions of this lightweight camera helped spur location shooting. [Courtesy of Carolina Production Services.]

cal technologies, such as transistors and new plastics and metal alloys, which permitted them to be strong, reliable, and lightweight.

The Arriflex 35BL camera, developed in Germany in the late 1960s, was so light and well balanced that it could easily be operated on a person's shoulder (see Figure 1.1). It was whisper quiet and delivered the highest-quality picture—as good as any of the larger cameras being produced at that time. Later versions of the 35BL are still heavily used today.

The Nagra sound recorder was not much larger than a shoebox and could easily be carried with a shoulder strap. Coupled with a new generation of lightweight, ultrasensitive "condenser" microphones, it matched the finest recording quality that could be achieved in the studio.

Initially, Hollywood paid little attention to these developments. Using a "bigger is better" strategy, it was fighting a battle

Figure 1.2 Cecomobile. This compact motion picture equipment truck, developed in the late 1960s, made it much easier to take lights, cameras, and sound gear on location.

with television with weapons that were even more gargantuan studio-bound technologies such as the three-camera Cinerama system, 70mm film stocks, and various 3-D technologies.

By the late 1960s, however, the American film establishment was beginning to change its ways, with the development of the Cinemobile in Hollywood and the Cecomobile in New York. The Cinemobile was a truck specifically designed for location shooting that would carry all the production equipment around from site to site in one little package. It was initially intended for the fledgling television production industry, which was trying to break out of the studio walls and get more visual interest within its tighter budgets.

The Cinemobile sported an ingenious system of storage cabinets for lighting, camera, and sound equipment in which the cabinets were arranged around its exterior, like little closets, for easy access (see Figure 1.2). The Cinemobile could be unloaded and repacked very quickly, with each department working out of its own storage cabinets and no one in anyone else's way.

Several Cinemobile designs even offered a dozen or so seats for the cast and crew. The entire company—fully equipped with all the lighting, camera, and sound gear it needed—could take off from the studio in the morning, spend the day filming, and return in the evening or perhaps spend the night in a motel and continue shooting on location the next day. There was no need to unpack or reinventory this remarkable little studio on wheels.

Working with cameras like the Arriflex 35BL, the Nagra recorder, and the Cinemobile was quite a change of pace from the big-studio, big–sound stage way of doing things. This filmmaking method instantly appealed to the new generation of young American directors who fell in love with the idea of breaking out of Hollywood's confines. It meshed perfectly with the vision of honest, real-life films that blossomed in the 1960s—including *Easy Rider, Midnight Cowboy, The Graduate,* and *The French Connection*—and TV shows like *Kojak* and *I Spy.* These productions reveled in a quick-paced, on-location, hip, and contemporary look and feel that were directly related to the ease of use of this new-generation equipment.

Today, even smaller, more lightweight, but very high-quality video and film technologies, such as Betacam SP and Super 16mm, have allowed a new generation to produce even faster-paced dramas, reality-based series, music videos, and globe-trotting documentaries. A half-hour show can contain scenes shot in twenty to thirty locations but still cost a fraction of the the amount required for a standard three- or four-set studio production.

Location shooting is now a large part of just about any motion picture production or still-photo shoot, regardless of budget or style. Although a number of factors account for this, the fundamental one is that directors and their audiences have come to demand the impressive, realistic touch that only an actual location can provide. Today, the location scouting and management field is larger than ever—and growing, as producers seek more interesting, different, and "perfect" locations that will keep an audience entertained.

WHAT IS A LOCATION?

A location is a real place. It is a specific structure, an area, or a setting where action and/or dialogue occurs in a script. As differentiated from a "set," a location is a place where a production must go in order to have the right background to tell its story. A location mentioned in a script can be very specific such as "the base of the Statue of Liberty," or very general such as "a cozy kitchen," or something purely imaginary such as "the planet Zargon." The location scout is the person who searches for the appropriate sites.

When writers, directors, and designers create their scenarios, they often have only an imaginary setting in mind. Although their vision of what they would like to see is clear in their mind, the corresponding setting may not actually exist. A writer generally does not preplan a story around a specific existing site such as "The Bowl-A-Rama, Statesville, North Carolina." He or she may remember a run-down bowling alley that was a wonderful childhood haunt, but chances are the bowling alley in question has disappeared, been irrevocably changed, or is 2,000 miles away.

The location scout's assignment is to find a place that is similar to what the writer has in mind and reasonably accessible to the production company in terms of both logistics and cost. It might be the real thing, but more often it is a suitable substitute that can be used to bring a writer's idea to life.

THE LOCATION SCOUT AND LOCATION MANAGER ROLES

A location scout's principal job is to submit photographs of possible locations. Once they are submitted, the scout's job is more or less complete. The location scout investigates certain broad logistical questions such as: How accessible is the location? Is the owner or tenant interested in having a shoot on the premises? Approximately how much money would he or she require as a fee? Are adequate electricity, parking, and other support services available? However, due to the great amount of searching required and the limited amount of time in which to do it, the scout usually cannot answer all the many questions that must be answered prior to making a final location selection. These questions are discussed in Chapter 4.

Once the locations have been selected, the location manager takes over. On a large production, there may be several location scouts reporting to one location manager. Depending on the number of locations needed, the tightness of the schedule, and unexpected production problems, the scout may be employed for the entire production or just the early preproduction period. With television commercials and other smaller, less complex productions, the location scout and manager are often the same person.

It makes sense for the scout to shift into the location manager position because he or she has done all the initial work. The only exception would be when a scout does not have a good background in production administration. Although the scout may be an expert in identifying suitable locations, it requires a significant leap in expertise to follow through with all the necessary arrangements that will guarantee a smooth shoot. On smaller shoots, in order to save money, the producer or production manager may take over all the location management responsibilities since there may not be enough work to justify the cost of having a location manager.

The location manager's chief concern is the handling of logistical and administrative chores required to ensure a smooth shoot. On larger shoots, there are thousands of details to attend to, so the location manager begins work in the earliest preproduction period and continues through the wrap. He or she negotiates all the details with the location's owners and/or tenants and researches both the situation in the neighborhood and government requirements and restrictions. All this must be done while balancing the needs of the production company with the needs of the location and the overall budgetary impact. The specifics of how this is accomplished are covered in Chapter 6.

THE CREATIVE INFLUENCE OF THE LOCATION PERSON

The location scout and manager have an undeniable influence on the creative direction of a production, occasionally as much as an art director or a costumer. Good location people must be well versed in production techniques and procedures. They must have good taste and a good design sense. They must be able to communicate with talented and creative individuals, to interpret subtleties and understand the themes that the writer and director are trying to convey.

The location person is actually at the forefront of the creative process—an extension of the eyes of the director, art director, and director of photography. What the scout chooses to notice or ignore will have a huge impact on the visual style of the production, so directors know that they must be able to trust the abilities of their scout. It can be an exciting position—one that provides great satisfaction when the scout is congratulated for finding the "perfect" site. There is no Academy Award for "Best Location," but good, smart location scouts are privately valued by the people who really count.

A LOCATION IS MORE THAN MEETS THE EYE

Although the look of a location is at least 75 percent of what determines its suitability, a scout must also address a number of other issues, covered in depth in Chapter 4. Basically, no matter how perfect a site appears to be, it may have large hidden problems that would prevent it from being a good candidate for a shooting location.

There can be problems in obtaining permission to use a property. It is not a good idea to assume that just because someone happens to own the perfect location, he or she will consent to allow it to be used for filming or photography. Many individuals, companies, and institutions wish to avoid public exposure or do not want to deal with the risks and activity that a shoot requires. Sometimes, the owner of a site is unreceptive because of a bad experience with a previous production.

On the other hand, the idea of having one's home or business used for a location can have a substantial glamorous appeal to more curious and adventurous people. Besides, shooting in such a site almost always involves a location fee, which can make a remarkable difference in anyone's attitude. Only the wealthiest would turn up their nose at a $1,000-a-day location fee, and a surprising number of the very rich will say yes in a heartbeat, too.

Even if permission can be obtained, there are many other reasons why a particular location might be unsuitable. It can be in a remote area or an unsuitable neighborhood, have unreliable roads, be too fragile or dangerous, have too many stairs or too busy a schedule. The list goes on and on.

It is important for a scout to keep these potential "unseen" problems in mind, and much of this book deals with how to avoid the thorny situations that can cause expensive production delays.

2

The Process of Scouting

THE SCOUTING ASSIGNMENT

Whether in film, television, or still photography, the location scout will receive a call initially from an administrator of the production—either the producer, the production manager, or the production coordinator. That staffer will need to determine the scout's availability and suitability for the assignment and discuss other business matters such as fees and expenses. A producer type will make this first call because there is no reason for a director to discuss creative details with a scout who is unavailable, unable to work within the schedule, or unfamiliar with the type of locations needed or whose fees are out of the production's budget range.

The producer and scout will briefly discuss the list of required locations, how long the scout feels it will take to find them, how long the producer has before the locations are needed, and how much the producer is willing to pay in location fees.

Sometimes, a scout may not be appropriate for a particular assignment. For example, a scout might have many, many connections for urban and suburban locations but never have scouted remote fishing villages. It is in the producer's best interest to find a scout with background and experience in the particular area where the shooting is to occur. If the scout has previously scouted an area—or better yet, has spent years living in it—he or she will have a much better idea of where to begin the search than someone new to the area and will likely accomplish the task much more quickly.

This initial conversation will usually be followed up immediately by a fax of the storyboard or script (discussed in the following section). Sometimes, the "boards" will be sent by express messenger, but increasingly, the speed of the fax is preferred and expected, so all serious scouts should own or have easy access to a fax machine. After the written material and/ or illustrations have been received, the scout will call back the production company to discuss any questions that are prompted by the material. All this can take place within a few hours, and the scout often will be out working, lining up and photographing potential sites, on the same day he or she receives the first phone call.

With feature films or other longer-form productions that might require anywhere from a dozen to a hundred locations, a complete script is sent, and the scout is given much more time to read and absorb the material. Feature-length productions require a long-term commitment lasting many months between the scout and the production company. On a feature film, an in-person interview is a necessity if the scout has not previously worked with the production team.

There is not a terrible sense of urgency for a large production, which usually has ample scouting time built into the schedule and budget. TV commercials and still-photo shoots are another story. They usually need their location yesterday, and scouting for commercials can become an exhausting, frantic race against a deadline imposed by an almost impossible airdate. Everyone agrees that there is something inherent about advertising that dictates last-minute decisions and rushed production schedules with horrendous deadlines. One must thrive in a fast-paced atmosphere to survive in the ad world.

THE SCRIPT AND STORYBOARD

The first and most basic tools of the location scout are the script and the storyboard. The *script* (see Figure 2.1) is the written form of the production created before any shooting is done. It can be drafted in many different formats, but it is essentially a description, in writing, of the action, settings, characters, and dialogue contained in a program.

The *storyboard* (see Figure 2.2) consists of individual illustrations of the action described in the script. It looks much like a comic strip, in which an artist has selected the essential information contained in a scene and drawn a picture of it. The storyboard and the script, together with the conversations with the producer and director, all give the scout a good idea of what is needed to fulfill the location requirements.

CONVERSATIONS WITH THE DIRECTOR

Although he or she may not be the first person to contact the scout, the director will always discuss the location requirements with the scout early in the scouting process, sometimes within minutes after the producer's initial phone call. During the course of the scout's conversation with the director, what was originally described in the script as "a large, scary house" becomes a more specific portrait of an isolated, four-story, mansard-roofed Victorian with lots of gingerbread detail, a rusting iron fence, a wraparound porch, and an ancient oak tree where a child's swing could be hung.

This process of focusing on the specific creative details provided by the director is critical for scouts, and it is important for them to take accurate notes for later reference. If the conversation can be tape-recorded for subsequent playback, so much the better, because every aspect of the description, even

TV/Radio Copy

TRAHAN, BURDEN & CHARLES, INC.
ADVERTISING AND PUBLIC RELATIONS

Date: May 24, 1993

Client: Maryland Lottery

Title: "It Could Be You" :30 TV

AUDIO	VIDEO
Let's say you're just walking along	TWO MEN PLAYING CHECKERS.
With a ticket in your pocket	
The next day you could be a millionaire	A WINNER ON LOADING DOCK.
With your own personal moon rocket.	
	PORSCHE DRIVE BY LOTTO SIGN.
CHORUS	BUS BY COUNTRY CAFE.
Everybody's got a dream	
And everyday	FARMER WATCHING SUNSET.
Somebody's dream comes true	
The Maryland Lottery	STEELWORKER GOING HOME.
It Could Be You	

TRAHAN, BURDEN & CHARLES, INC.   ADVERTISING AND PUBLIC RELATIONS   1030 NORTH CHARLES ST., BALTIMORE, MD 21201-5402   410-347-7500

Figure 2.1   Shooting script for a 30-sec. TV commercial. [Courtesy of Trahan, Burden and Charles, Inc., Advertising and Public Relations.]

Figure 2.2 Storyboard for a 30-sec. TV commercial. A location scout will use this as an important guide to the sort of location a producer is seeking. [Courtesy of Trahan, Burden and Charles, Inc., Advertising and Public Relations.]

every adjective, will provide scouts with valuable leads about what will ultimately please the director.

DEALING WITH THE PRODUCER VERSUS THE DIRECTOR

Depending on the size of the production, the scout may also occasionally speak with an art director or a designer to obtain even more creative input and suggestions. However, at this point, the scout will usually deal primarily with the producer or production manager. The main reason for this is that the producer must examine all the effects of a location choice—including factors affecting budget, schedule, and logistics—not just creative considerations.

Given the nature of the director's job, he or she concentrates on how a particular location choice will affect the story or theme of the production and may not be as concerned about budget, schedule, and logistics. Therefore, before submitting the choices to the director, the producer will often want to screen out some options that might look appealing but would be inappropriate for budgetary or administrative reasons. The producer would not want the director to consider a location that is out of the budget range (e.g., a distant site that would involve too much travel)—first, because he or she does not want to waste the director's time, and second, because it is politically unwise to offer an apparently attractive possibility and then take it away. If the director is presented with inappropriate options, he or she might latch onto an overly difficult or expensive location, which could become a source of friction for everyone.

LOCATION RESOURCES

Requests for locations can range from a picturesque meadow to a classic small town to the interior of a nineteenth-century factory to a superhighway to a coal mine and literally thousands more. No matter how extensive the scout's experience, he or she will never have a ready-made list of possibilities at hand.

There are simply too many types of locations, and it will take a lot of thought and research to find the "perfect" one.

Certain locations—such as kitchens, offices, and middle-class homes—do tend to recur, but even then, there is a huge variety of styles from which to choose. Although an experienced scout will have some good ideas from past scouting expeditions, he or she can usually count on the need to go out and seriously search for something brand-new.

Once the scout understands what sort of site is required, there are a number of resources that can help him or her discover these new locations. Some are specifically designed to assist professional location persons, and others are simply commonsense approaches. What follows is a survey of the best possibilities.

LOCATION COMPANIES

In many of the larger production centers around the country—such as New York, Los Angeles, Chicago, and Miami—there are companies that deal only with locations. Most have been started by persons who have, through years of scouting, been able to assemble a variety of location owners who are happy to offer their premises to production crews. These locations are prephotographed, preapproved, and prepriced for shooting. Location companies maintain extensive photo files of perhaps thousands of locations, and they can be a gold mine for the location scout.

A location company basically acts as an agent or a broker for location owners. In some cases, persons interested in having their homes used as locations will contact a location company. The company then photographs the houses and adds them to its collection. In other cases, the location company builds its collection from ongoing experience with desirable locations and willing owners. Location companies charge both a rental fee for the location and a commission for themselves, which is either a flat fee or a percentage, depending on the particular company. Most location companies are happy to do custom scouting as well.

Besides supplying extensive photos of the sites it offers, a good location company will also have noted many helpful details about each location, such as parking, access to utilities, room measurements, and elevator access. Of course, it always sets the price, which is negotiable, like everything in the production business. Other advantages of using a location company are that it is fast and there are few unanswered questions. In an hour of searching through the company's albums or files, a scout can get a detailed look at dozens of likely prospects.

Location companies do have some drawbacks, however. First, they *are* competition for an independent scout, and the scout should consider, frankly, whether a location company might try to steal the client. Also, a producer, having hired the scout as an independent, might be miffed that the scout is "subcontracting" and thereby taking an easier, more expensive route.

When there is a good relationship between an independent scout and a location company, the location company will usually give the independent a discount, in hopes that he or she will return with more business. In any case, it costs nothing to look. If a location company's client is not chosen, there is no charge. If the perfect location is found at the right price, no one will care how it was selected.

Location companies can have a fairly limited stock of choices. Since most print and TV advertising is for consumer products used in the home, private homes are in the greatest demand as locations, and the average location company will specialize in that type of site. It would be unusual to find a steel mill or pig farm in the pristine pages of most location companies' photo albums.

For example, Bergen County, New Jersey, just across the Hudson River from New York City, is known as the "Kitchen Capital of the World" because its comfortable, all-American, upscale homes have appeared in countless print ads and TV commercials for the giant food and soap companies whose ad agencies are headquartered in Manhattan. More than a few location companies in the New York metropolitan area specialize in this sort of suburban home.

Another drawback to using a location company is that its locations can often be overused. A location company's best classic suburban home exteriors or kitchens might appear in ten different commercials every year, and a scout must be careful to avoid duplication. Although a location can be redecorated to a certain extent, the scout must be aware of other recent uses of a company's locations.

Perhaps the greatest drawback to using location companies is their cost. A location company requires significant overhead, usually much higher than an independent scout's because working out of a home is less expensive; they must spend money to maintain an office and advertise. Therefore, they are geared primarily for the TV commercial and print ad markets, which have the highest budgets, and their rates reflect this, with fees of $1,500 to $2,000 per day plus commission as a minimum. Although that is reasonable for a national TV spot, it would give fits to the production manager of a low-budget TV movie. Producers on tight budgets hope that by using an independent scout, they will be able to uncover a good but lower-priced location. Sometimes, they are right.

Nevertheless, most location companies have worked hard to find their clients. Their selections are excellent and generally carefree. The owners represented by location companies know what it is like to have a production crew crawling all over their property for fourteen hours a day and feel they are being adequately compensated by the location fee. With a location company, preproduction and shooting are handled on a very professional level, so the shooting is rarely disrupted by unpleasant surprises from unhappy owners or disturbed neighbors.

Finally, the location company business is extremely volatile, and companies come and go quickly. Location scouting is a tiny niche business, which makes it quite risky. It takes a lot of energy to maintain a good collection of up-to-date files, and if a certain company's stock of locations goes out of fashion or becomes overused, or if the current vogue in advertising turns to studio shooting and animation, a location company can run out of steam fast.

FILM COMMISSIONS

The local film commission is a good first stop in most scouting situations. In the 1970s, only the largest production centers—such as New York City, Los Angeles, and Chicago—had official agencies whose sole purpose was to attract and assist TV producers, film producers, and still photographers. However, the general economic boom of the 1980s spread to the film industry as well, with film commissions becoming a national vogue among state and local governments.

Producers of all sorts began to roam the country shooting feature films, documentaries, industrial films, TV spots, TV movies, and music videos. TV commercial advertising and budgets mushroomed during that period, allowing producers to look well beyond their own backyards for the perfect location. Suddenly, areas such as Atlanta, Washington-Baltimore, Jacksonville, Seattle, and the Carolinas woke up to the fact that production after production was being shot in their midst.

The general impression among government public relations moguls is that the movie industry is beneficial—that motion pictures have multimillion-dollar budgets, which producers will spend with abandon in the local economy. Production is seen as a clean, high-tech industry that makes few demands on public services. Movie producers are generally delighted to pay police officers, fire fighters, and other government workers overtime rates for their help and cooperation. Having a movie or TV show shot in an area is exciting for the government. It generates upbeat stories for the press, provides a boosterish cause for politicians, and creates pride among the citizens—somewhat akin to the town winning a beauty contest.

The word of mouth about this wonderful new industry of location filmmaking spread quickly throughout the United States. A certain amount of me-tooism flourished, with even counties and small towns feeling that since their neighbor sported a film commission, they should have one, too. Sometimes, just a single TV movie was enough to stimulate the formation of a film commission in a small city, and many have targeted location production as a growth industry.

Every state in the union now has some sort of permanent film commission (see Appendix A). These commissions meet at various location expos to discuss all the new trends in attracting productions, including toll-free hot lines, huge still-photo libraries, promotional videos, free scouting, and more. At these expos, film commissioners boast about how many million production dollars came into their area, where their state ranks in amount of production, or someone's tentative plans to shoot a multimillion-dollar epic in their hometown sometime soon.

Film Commission Services

A film commission generally offers a standard menu of services to producers. Funded by its local government, the film commission is primarily a marketing tool used to bring productions into an area, so its services are free. The quality of those services depends heavily on the size of the budget, which can vary greatly from one commission to another. Besides marketing the state's production capabilities to producers, the film commission usually offers the following services:

- *Publication of a production guide:* This is a directory, often consisting of a hundred or more pages, that lists companies and individuals serving the production industry. Although such guides can be inaccurate, incomplete, or out of date, they are usually of some help. Some states offer free listings; others charge people and companies to be included. The ones that charge are less complete since the average support person sees little value in marketing and will not spend the $20 to $40 fee to be listed in a guide.
- *Advice and help in finding locations:* Most film commission people are natives of their area and can offer many leads for possible locations. Commissions often will

provide free scouting services for larger productions. Most commissions have small staffs, and when busy, they may not be of much assistance in this area.

- *A still-photo file of a wide range of locations:* The better film commissions maintain large files of stills and/or videos of prescouted locations, which usually include commonly requested sites such as jails, hospitals, offices, parks, and small towns or large cities. Scouts who want to familiarize themselves with the flavor of an area will find these files very helpful.

- *Assistance in obtaining official permits and dealing with other government agencies, community groups, and merchant associations:* Film commissions are often given a mandate by the governor's office to provide the utmost assistance to producers and can therefore cut through red tape quickly.

These resources are important tools for location scouts, allowing them to cover a lot of ground quickly. Plus, the fact that the film commission's services are free can represent a significant savings to the production budget.

However, the location scout/manager should remember that each film is unique, that no film commission (regardless of its claims) will have had experience with all possible types of production, and that sometimes a film commission will simply be unable to cut through the bureaucratic maze that constitutes most governments. In short, the film commission cannot automatically be counted on to deliver whatever a production may need.

Finally, the location scout/manager must be aware that film commissions are primarily concerned with marketing. Many will tout their "complete services," but when it comes to delivering, they simply do not have the power or position to provide everything a production needs. Unfortunately, once a production has been landed, the film commission may be more concerned about landing another than serving the one it has. In the vast majority of cases, a commission should be among the scout's first contacts. Just be aware of the limitations.

LOCAL SOURCES OF ASSISTANCE

There are other good, sometimes better than film commissions, sources for location leads. Their services are free, and they usually are all quite happy to help a scout.

Local Governments

In small towns or counties, and even in many larger cities that do not have a film commission, there is often an office on the local level that can assist location scouts—usually an office of tourism, business development, or public information. In very small towns, the mayor's office can handle inquiries and production needs quite satisfactorily, opening many doors—often better than some big-city film commissions. It may take several tries to connect with someone who has the desire and ability to help, but once that person is found, he or she can be immensely useful.

Many of the better film commissions have a network of contacts already set up in local governments throughout their state. This is a good reason why a state's film commission should be called first. If the commission does not happen to have a contact in a particular locale, then it is usually happy to find one, using the state agency's influence to lend an air of officiality to the requests of a stranger.

Chambers of Commerce

In areas where there is no film commission or the film commission provides little assistance in logistical situations, there is usually a chamber of commerce that will be glad to help with most reasonable requests. A chamber of commerce is an association of local business owners whose unabashed and commendable goal is to make it easy for people to spend money in their businesses. Generally, even the smallest town will have a chamber.

Chamber of commerce members are well connected with the movers and shakers in an area, including real estate brokers, government officials, and any sort of business. They can be helpful in providing personal introductions and opening doors to individuals and organizations that might not be receptive to cold calling by a stranger. A chamber's cooperation grants an official seal of approval to a location person and will save time, money, and headaches in the long run.

If the phone directory lists no chamber of commerce, all the scout needs to do is ask at the local businesses. In some extremely small towns, the chamber might be a rather informal group that lacks a full-time staff or office and simply breakfasts together once a week in the local café, but its members will still be a friendly and helpful bunch.

Community Associations

In some scouting situations, approaching the local community or neighborhood association can be the most effective way to find certain locations. This is especially true when the scout is looking for private residences—a tricky task, given most people's reluctance to open their homes to strangers. Like chamber of commerce members, people who are active in community associations are usually well-connected, well-respected, and outgoing individuals. If a location scout merely knocks on strangers' doors asking whether they would like to have their home appear on television and would they mind having detailed photographs taken of it, the doors will probably be shut in the scout's face. But if the scout is accompanied by someone from the community association, those doors will probably be opened.

Because they know their neighbors very well, heads of community associations can help the scout screen out especially suspicious or otherwise unsuitable owners of potential locations. They will know who would be happy to put up with a little disruption in exchange for a location fee—the younger couple who could use the extra cash, the woman who is an amateur actress, the retired man who is a real movie buff, and so forth. These community association members are always volunteers, and a good scout will offer them some pay as compensation for their time and effort. They are certainly worth it because their personal connections will often get a scout better and faster results than anyone else could.

Heads of community associations can be fairly easy to find. Many counties require that all associations register with the local clerk of the court. The addresses and phone numbers of the associations' officers are a matter of public record and will be given to anyone who asks at the clerk's office. If a particular neighborhood does not have a registered association, then the next best approach is to knock on the doors of several homes and ask whether there is a community association and whom to contact. This is usually a safe question that will not arouse suspicion. The scout should start with the neatest, best-maintained house on the block. It is likely to be a member of an association if one exists.

One note of caution about community associations: Sometimes, they can be run by self-appointed "community guardians" who are merely busybodies disliked by the entire neighborhood. A simple guide to follow is: If the person is open and helpful, he or she will have the support and friendship of many neighbors; if the person is tense and skeptical, then the scout should continue looking around the neighborhood for a more likable person who will have more friends.

A final suggestion: Many community association leaders from different communities know each other and will gladly pass on each other's names. This can save a lot of time if one community proves unsuitable for a shoot and the scout needs to look at others.

Area Guides and Books

In larger locales, visiting a local bookstore will usually reward the scout with a well-stocked rack containing an area's picture guide and local history books. The local library, whether small or large, will often dedicate a shelf exclusively to books about its area. There might be an elegant coffee table book about local mansions, which would be an excellent resource if a scout were looking for sites of that type. There will usually be a history book of any given area with illustrations of its most interesting and picturesque structures and settings.

In larger cities or other areas with even small tourist industries, general guidebooks are indispensable tools that can reveal new facts even to lifelong natives. They will provide lots of information in a concise format and may cover businesses, residences, historical sites, architectural gems, recreational areas, and many other potential locations. They are usually illustrated with maps and list phone numbers, hours of operation, and contact names.

The local government offices will often have business development or tourism brochures listing various useful sites and resources, and the scout should load up with all the printed matter available there. Not only might these brochures contain useful scouting information, but they will be even more important as a source of information about the availability of support services such as hotels, restaurants, taxis, stationers, and so on, should the production company eventually come to the area.

OTHER PEOPLE'S HELP

With the possible exception of the head of the community association and a few guidebooks, it should be repeated that all these supports are absolutely free. A good scout will have a network of state-level, regional, local, and community-based people working for her or him early in the project. These people may not always be productive, but the beauty of this approach is that they are basically working for the scout, extending her or his research abilities many times over for only the effort of a few short phone calls.

These individuals and their organizations are happy to help and know the territory. They can accomplish a hundred times what a scout could by driving through unfamiliar neighborhoods and knocking on strangers' doors. If a scout is looking for a dairy farm, for example, all he or she needs to do is phone the local agricultural agent, who will usually be happy to call around to a dozen farmers and then get back to the scout with the best possibilities. This could save days of work.

Consequently, a scout must have a nose for quality research and an ability to organize and manage resources so that they will multiply his or her effectiveness. Sometimes, a scout can almost sit back and let his or her initial contacts do the work. But then again, usually not. Most often, it is a combination of good connections and determined prospecting that enables the scout to discover the perfect location.

Burned Bridges

One final but important suggestion for utilizing various resources is that care must be taken to treat everyone with respect and to act with integrity. Unfortunately, quite a few production companies have misused the assistance provided to them by municipalities and other government agencies or community associations. Many neighborhoods around the country now specifically prohibit media production because of the disruption it is felt to have caused in the past.

In some cases, disruption may be unavoidable, and a great fuss can be made by a small, overly sensitive, if not mean-spirited group (or even an individual) over what are in reality small inconveniences. In other cases, though, production companies may be insensitive and overzealous about their demands and create situations that are genuine nuisances, bordering on harassment.

When the public is mistreated, the entire production industry suffers. A government agency will be reluctant to deal with location scouts who want to go into neighborhoods where production company activities have generated complaints in the past.

People who have had bad experiences with production crews automatically will be suspicious of other productions. When scouts come upon one of these situations, they must be careful to assure the concerned parties that their production company will honor its commitments and respect the needs and concerns of the public. Not all productions burn their bridges, and scouts must be prepared to convince leery residents or associations that their particular company will act responsibly.

For a large production, this might even require the scout's addressing a town council or community group to convince its members that the production company will honor all its promises. A serious, responsible presentation must be made in order to gain trust and cooperation. The location person cannot be shy or have any qualms about getting up in front of a group and persuading them to accept a production.

Above all, the scout must see that his or her promises are kept by the production company. If the scout and the production company have handled a location shoot properly, they should be able to leave with sincere letters of commendation from the location owner, neighbors, and local officials. These are good references for the future and will place that scout in a different class from those who employ the "slash-and-burn" production style.

THE CAR AS AN OFFICE

Location scouts must be out and about to such an extent that they virtually live in their car. Over the course of a feature film, scouts can expect to put 6,000 miles on their car, spending ten to twelve hours a day driving around looking for possibilities or following up leads.

Working out of a car involves its own routines, many of which might seem pretty strange to most office workers, factory workers, and others based indoors. A location scout's workday actually has a lot in common with the perhaps less glamorous daily grind of real estate brokers, taxi drivers, truck drivers, delivery people, or outside salespeople. Basic activities, such as eating lunch, finding a rest room, or getting a drink of water, take on a new dimension when one is tied to a car in a strange area for ten or more hours.

Taking Care of Oneself

At the most basic level, simply finding a rest room becomes an important task after scouts have ridden in a car for several hours. Many gas stations, particularly in urban areas, are rapidly eliminating their rest rooms. Also, just because a station says it has a rest room does not mean the facility will be in working order. Scouts in need of a pit stop must take a moment to check out the rest room *before* pumping their gas; otherwise, they might be sorely disappointed. The only reliable source for rest rooms is fast-food outlets; they rarely have mean signs declaring "For Customers Only."

Since scouts might be having all three daily meals on the road, eating properly becomes a challenge. The vast majority of roadside restaurants are now some sort of fast-food franchise. Aside from the questionable health implications of a steady diet of hamburgers and fried chicken, having fast food three times a day can get pretty boring. Also, eating in one strange restaurant after another invites all sorts of stomach ailments, which could make any scouting trip a dismal affair.

The simple solution is for scouts to accept the fact that they will be on the road all day long and take five minutes in the morning to make up a sandwich and pack a few pieces of fruit, some healthy drinks, and snacks. Location scouting is a sedentary occupation, and the lure of junk food is everywhere. Scouts are much better off with a small cooler packed with healthy food and drinks. It is easier on the pocketbook too.

As for other basic vehicle needs, they do not differ significantly from the usual auto comforts. But scouts must realize that they will be spending eight to twelve hours a day in the car, which is much different from a standard commute. A good radio/cassette or radio/CD player will make long drives pass more quickly. Having a dependable, safe, and sound vehicle is an absolute must, and if it is equipped with four-wheel drive, so much the better, because this will prove handy both for wintery weather and off-road situations. Good interior lights for reading maps after dark are important.

Radar detectors, though not a permit for reckless driving and illegal in some jurisdictions, might be justifiable since scouts drive so much on unfamiliar roads where there is a good possibility of encountering unfair speed traps. The amount of time scouts spend driving substantially increases their odds of being involved in an accident or getting a ticket, so safe, alert driving is critical. A CB radio is a good idea to help scouts avoid traffic jams, get emergency help, and maybe provide some entertainment on a long drive. Membership in any of the national auto clubs provides many beneficial emergency road services, including free maps, free towing, hot-shot starts, and locked-door opening. This is a good basic package, and as scouts spend more time in the car, their personal preferences will become obvious.

Scouts will find it imperative to carry a spare set of keys in a wallet or hidden in a little magnetic box somewhere on the *exterior* of the car. Nothing is more frustrating than foolish delays caused by losing car keys or locking them inside the car. And because scouts rush in and out of their car perhaps fifty times a day, with a hundred things on their mind, a lockout *will* eventually occur. Finally, in unfamiliar areas, cars should not be allowed to get too low on gas; there's no telling where the next station will be.

Many would regard the preceding advice as basic common sense, but it indicates that a location scout/manager must be a detail-oriented professional. Making lame excuses for dumb mistakes will not solve problems or impress anyone.

Keeping in Touch on the Road

Using the car for an office presents other unique challenges. Above all, location scouts must always be reachable by the production office for additional instructions, updates, and important messages. There are several ways to keep in touch with the world, including cellular phones, electronic pagers, and roadside pay phones. The best-prepared scouts use all three, expensive as they might be.

Although cellular phones are wonderful, they have a few drawbacks. First, they can be quite expensive. Monthly bills of over $1,000 are not uncommon, but they can be avoided with sensible use. Second, there are still many, many areas where reception is nonexistent or at best spotty, rendering a cellular phone useless. Even in well-covered cellular areas, the vagaries of cellular radio waves do not guarantee anything like landline telephone reliability, and most regular cellular users find that their phones will not work a significant percentage of the time. Finally, scouts who plan to use a cellular phone on production business should first ask the company whether it will pay the bill. It is not a good idea to present a production manager with a surprise $250 cellular phone bill.

Pagers are a more reliable method for staying in contact. Furthermore, they cost an average of only $20 per month—and often much less—which is a big plus. Although they are a less immediate form of communication, they are lightweight and much easier to carry than most cellular phones. Some models offer a silent vibrating alert and digital display, making them excellent for shooting situations in which silence is required. Pagers generally have a much greater range of reception than cellular phones and are not subject to interference from buildings and other objects. There are also several companies that offer nearly complete national coverage with their pager systems, something that is still fairly cumbersome and expensive to achieve with cellular phones.

The basic pay phone, while the most reliable type of communication, is not quite what it used to be before telephone system deregulation. Many small entrepreneurs have entered the pay phone business offering poor-quality units with inadequate long-distance service. The obvious drawback to depending on the pay phone for staying in contact is that scouts must regularly stop and find one to use. Pay phones are exposed to bad weather and loud street noise and may lack a convenient writing surface. They can be out of order or have a line of people waiting to use them. They can be on a bad corner in a bad neighborhood, or there may not be one for 20 miles.

On the other hand, a well-located, good-quality pay phone can be the most electronically reliable—and by far the cheapest—communications tool of all. As scouts become familiar with a particular area, they get to know the locations of the best pay phones. There are a number of sources that can be counted on for good pay phones. Hotel and motel lobbies usually have spacious banks of sheltered, reliable telephones and are the best bet. They have plenty of close parking for quick in-and-out visits. Office buildings, public libraries, post offices, and better restaurants are also good candidates for having safe, quiet, easily accessible, and out-of-the-weather phone booths. Finally, just about every convenience store has a bank of pay phones that are easy to drive up to and well lighted, if not very well sheltered from noise or weather.

Gas station pay phones are the last choice because, even if they are working, they are usually stuck on an outside pole, exposed to weather and noise, and will usually have the worst off-brand phone unit and the lousiest long-distance carrier. It is the corporate policy of many fast-food franchises not to have pay phones because they do not want to attract people who need to use a phone, only those who want to eat, so forget about combining phone calls and pit stops.

It is worth repeating that it is absolutely essential for a scout to be constantly in touch and reachable. On any production, situations can change rapidly, and those changes must be communicated immediately. To be taken seriously as a professional, the scout must at least have a pager with a digital LCD (where the caller's number is displayed). This does the least damage to the pocketbook too.

The best high-tech communications system is a home answering machine that includes a feature to auto-dial a pager or cellular phone. When a message comes in, the home answering machine dials the pager. Having received the page, the scout calls the home machine on his or her transportable cellular phone (a high-wattage model that can be carried from car to car), retrieves the message, and then returns the call in less than three minutes. Of course, the scout also could be available directly by both cellular phone and pager, and can decide which number to give out to whom, thereby managing his or her "reachability." Giving out a cellular phone number to everyone may result in a lot of nuisance calls that must be paid for at cellular rates. That can get expensive.

TOOLS OF THE LOCATION SCOUT
AND LOCATION MANAGER

Besides the car and phone, location scouts require any number of smaller tools, as in the following list, to do their job. Some of these additional items are necessities; others simply make the work go more smoothly. Many of them are used by the location manager only during the production phase, but it does no harm to go over them at this point. They will all fit into a car, and they will be used often.

- *35mm still camera*: The requirements for this camera are discussed in Chapter 3.
- *Polaroid camera*: A Polaroid is optional if a 35mm camera is used.
- *Video camcorder*: Some producers prefer video camcorders, which are discussed in detail in Chapter 3.
- *Complete set of area road maps*: Good quality maps are more readily available for some areas than they are for others. County maps and town/city maps are best; state maps are not very useful because they lack a lot of necessary detail.
- *Compass*: The best type is a liquid-filled model. Its importance is covered in Chapter 3.

- *Change pouch and coins*: A heavy-duty pouch can be used to hold coins for pay phones, parking meters, and road tolls. Quarters are the most commonly needed coin, and scouts can use as many as twenty to fifty of them a day.
- *Flashlight*: One that is good and reliable, but not too heavy, will come in handy for night work, going into unlit basements or buildings, and looking at fuse boxes.
- *Measuring tape*: This is used to measure doorways, ceiling heights, gate clearances, window openings, and much more.
- *Pocket weather radio*: This enables the location person to keep abreast of the latest weather details.
- *Portable office*: This can consist of a hanging-file box with space for pencils, scissors, markers, paper clips, ruler, hole punch, and other office supplies.
- *Surveyor's ribbon*: This neon-bright plastic ribbon is good for blocking off parking spaces or marking areas for crowd control. It also can be tied to telephone poles as route markers.
- *Traffic cones*: These short, bright orange cones are used to mark parking places or to alert vehicles to slow down. The transportation department usually has them, but the location person should keep one or two in the car trunk for emergencies.
- *Car battery jumper cables*: The location person is usually the first in and last out of a shooting site, and these cables will be used to give a hot shot at least once in every production. Be prepared!
- *Business cards*: Simple but official-looking cards make the location person look like a trustworthy professional in the eyes of most strangers. They open many doors.
- *Copies of insurance certificates*: Owners of potential locations are comforted by these official documents, which describe the production company's various liability insurance policies. (See Chapter 7.)

- *Show cards*: These 2-foot × 3-foot pieces of white cardboard are good for making signs to parking areas or asking passersby to be quiet. The grip truck will have them on the shoot day, but the location person would be well advised to carry half a dozen for making signs early in the morning before anyone else arrives.
- *Supersize permanent markers*: These are used for writing on the show cards.
- *Basic hand-tool kit*: The contents should include a hammer, wire cutter, screwdrivers, adjustable wrenches, pliers, and small saws. An inadvertently locked gate may need to be opened quickly, and the production must not be delayed because a $2 hasp cannot be broken. Any damage can be repaired later, if need be.
- *Rain gear*: An umbrella, a rainsuit, and galoshes are a big help. On the inevitable rainy days, the location department does not stop work, and a day with wet feet is a day spent in misery. Be prepared. Always carry rain gear (unless working in a desert!).
- *Carryall with shoulder strap*: This bag should be large enough to hold a lot of the stuff listed here and more, while leaving the hands free to write notes or make phone calls.
- *Binoculars*: These can come in handy, especially when scouting from a boat or an aircraft.

These items will make the work easier. They also will make the scout look professional in the eyes of the producer. A director will be impressed when the scout pulls out a compass or measuring tape in response to a question. Something as simple as a pocket weather radio is a slick, impressive tool that is really practical too.

One final item: When the scout is riding around with the other people on the production staff, having a cooler filled with a good selection of drinks and a few snacks in the trunk or back seat of a van will please even the most jaded director, director of photography, or producer. They will be sincerely grateful for some quality refreshments throughout a long scouting day, and it will save time by not having to stop repeatedly at convenience stores.

3

Photo-Documenting
the Location

THE IMPORTANCE OF STILL PHOTOGRAPHY

The camera, in its many versions, is the most important tool of location scouts. Many types of camera are used, from cardboard throwaways to near broadcast-quality video, but all have the same purpose—to show a production team what scouts have found. Scouts need not be ace photographers, but the better their photos, the more respect they will gain.

Because the camera is the scouts' most important tool, it is imperative that they have some hands-on experience with still-photo techniques. Taking a photography course and spending some serious hours practicing prior to marketing their skills professionally will give scouts a valuable foundation in getting adequate, if not good, photos.

On a location-scouting expedition, photographing is a fast-paced operation. Scouts have a lot of ground to cover and cannot spend a long time composing a shot or adjusting equipment.

They must make a keen appraisal of their subject, capture its essence, and then move on, assured that they have taken some good photographs. The style is comparable to that of a photojournalist who is working on deadline. Scouting sometimes even requires shooting from moving cars, boats, and airplanes or through windows and fences.

The scouts' main goal is to offer a range of choices to a production team, not to create a beautiful study of one or two sites. If there is an interest in a location, more time can be spent later going back for a closer look and maybe more detailed photo coverage. Because only a small percentage of photographed locations are actually used, anything more than a quick, concise photo study is a waste of time. The exception, of course, is when scouts find the "perfect" location. Then they can be excused for taking a bit more time to get the best shots. Perfect locations, however, are quite rare, and good scouts will temper their use of time, energy, and film with good judgment.

POLAROID CAMERAS

Not too many years ago, the Polaroid was the camera of choice for photographing locations. Its instant picture-processing technology made it the perfect tool to use when a location had to be scouted quickly and photos had to be presented at a meeting or shipped cross-country within several hours. This was before the era of the ubiquitous one-hour 35mm print-processing machines, when even the fastest lab required 24 hours to develop and print stills. The Polaroid's instant, easy-to-use technology was one of the modern wonders—and was employed for many purposes by people in the business of making images, particularly location scouts.

The Polaroid, however, has a few significant drawbacks and limitations when compared with other still cameras. First, it offers only one lens, which photographs in an odd ratio that does not match any of the standard motion picture image ratios. Second, its general photographic quality is mediocre to poor compared with 35mm stills when considering contrast ratio, color reproduction, and sensitivity in dim light. Polaroids use a slow film that requires a flash in any interior situation.

Furthermore, they only work well at fairly standard room temperatures because of the film's delicate integral chemistry. Outside, on a cold day, Polaroids have a lot of color problems and may produce no image at all. Polaroid prints cannot be duplicated easily or quickly with any quality. They are also rather delicate and cannot be cropped or cut in any way without leaking messy chemicals and ruining the image.

Finally, Polaroid film is expensive, and few stores stock the best-quality emulsions. There are also different types of Polaroid film, and the best types may not work in all Polaroid cameras, so the user must always keep plenty of acceptable quality on hand. That can be an expensive proposition, since Polaroid film averages about $1 per shot and can spoil in a comparatively short time.

THE ONE-HOUR PHOTO LAB

A solution to the difficulties with Polaroid film arrived in the mid-1980s with the introduction of the one-hour 35mm photo-developing/printing machines. These remarkable units provide many benefits: the wonderful photographic quality of fine-grained 35mm film and a variety of raw stocks, including high speeds of more than 1000 ASA, which can handle even candlelit scenes without a flash. In one hour, labs can use these machines to make two or even three crisp copies of every shot in a variety of print sizes, including a remarkable 4 × 6-inch size—the size preferred by producers and directors because it brings out so much detail.

DESIRABLE CAMERA FEATURES

To be suitable for scouting use, a 35mm camera should be a good-quality single-lens reflex model. It should be simple enough to use quickly and offer the choice of fully automatic exposure and focus or fully manual control. The automatic controls are lifesavers when scouts need to shoot quickly from a moving car or an airplane. At other times, a tricky, difficult-to-light interior shot or a strongly backlit exterior shot must be taken, so manual controls will be needed to obtain a high-quality, useful photo.

Inexpensive, all-automatic cameras with self-threading and rewinding motors are popular with amateurs but are a source of trouble because they are prone to unexpected failure. It is disastrous to return from a long scouting trip only to discover that all the shots are black or severely out of focus due to a malfunctioning camera. Scouting is an expensive proposition for a producer, and the time and money invested in it should not be risked because the scout is using a cheap, unreliable camera. A good professional or semipro camera is the only choice for scouts who want to be respected as professionals. Scouts who are using a camera that costs less than $150 are using the wrong camera.

All 35mm still cameras offer the important feature of allowing the photographer to change lenses when a different focal length is needed. The standard lens size for a 35mm camera is the 50mm lens, which basically mimics the perspective of the human eye. A wider-angle lens of 25mm or no more than 35mm can be very helpful in a small room where the normal 50mm lens simply cannot include the desired field of view from one angle.

Zoom lenses offer a choice of focal lengths, from wide to telephoto, eliminating the bother of changing lenses, but they are large and can be a bit bulky for quick-moving scouts who need to jockey their camera in and out of a carrying case all day long. Because they utilize more layers of optical glass, zooms are slower too—that is, they transmit less light. This only becomes a problem at the end of the day when the sun is going down or in interiors where a flash is either inappropriate or not allowed. Although fast, compact zooms can be found, they are much more expensive than a suitable two-lens combination.

For scouts who do not mind changing the lens just occasionally, the best solution is to have a normal 50mm lens plus a 28mm lens to use when a wider field of view is needed. The 50mm lens is preferred for a number of reasons (discussed later in this chapter) and will be used exclusively in 70 to 80 percent of scouting situations.

There are pros and cons to using the autofocus feature offered on certain cameras. Again, in some quickly changing situations, it can be a great help, but the autofocus mechanism can be fooled often enough to ruin important shots. It is better to take the extra few seconds to focus manually, and be sure that the photos are as clear as they need to be, than to risk soft-focus shots that will be irritating to anyone studying the location stills. Finally, autofocus is just another hard-to-repair device that can fail at the wrong moment, causing headaches, wasted time, and money.

CAMERA ACCESSORIES

Although a camera tripod might be useful occasionally, scouts are normally moving too fast to take the time to set one up properly. A flash unit, however, is a necessity and will eliminate the need for a tripod in most situations. The flash should be of good quality: a quick-recycling model that can be adjusted for bounce flashes. Bounce flashes provide a much more pleasing light for interior shots and mimic the soft, indirect lighting style of the best photographers and cinematographers. Once again, to avoid slowing their work, scouts should choose the smallest flash model available that still offers the aforementioned features.

Another good accessory is the camera bag, which should be large enough to hold any additional lenses, several rolls of film, the flash unit, and a few other small supplies. The bag helps keep the camera kit safe and dry, but most important, it enables scouts to store everything in one place so they will always have just what they need right at hand.

EXPENDABLE STILL-PHOTO SUPPLIES

Although scouts do not require all the gadgets of professional photographers, their camera bag should contain simple items such as lens-cleaning fluid and tissues. Much more important, cameras and flash units run on batteries, and because scouts can go through ten or more rolls of film a day, their camera batteries will run down faster than those of the normal amateur. Scouts would be wise to stock their camera bag with several spares for *all* the various types of batteries that their camera system needs. This is particularly true in the case of the dime-size camera batteries, which come in many varieties and may not be easy to obtain at the local convenience shop or drugstore. Spare batteries also should be kept on hand for the flash attachment, which usually requires the readily available AA or AAA size. Remember, no battery ever died at a convenient time, so scouts must be prepared!

It is imperative for scouts to have enough still-photo stock at all times. Because the requirements for such stock are considered in more detail in the following subsection, it will suffice at this point to observe that since 35mm film is cheap and light enough for scouts to carry a dozen rolls, there is no excuse for running out during a critical shoot when the nearest store is 20 miles away and only a few minutes of good daylight are left.

Still-Photo Stock

Dozens of types of 35mm film stocks are available in a great range of prices. Although scouts can go with the most expensive brand, even the least expensive is adequate for location stills. Between brands, there can be a price difference of as much as $2 to $3 per roll, which can add hundreds of extra dollars to the cost of a scout. Steadily working scouts will use dozens of rolls per month, so it is advisable to stock up at the near-wholesale prices offered by most discount stores. Some one-hour photo labs even give a roll of totally adequate "house-brand" film stock free with every roll processed. It is usually a good deal and saves scouts from having to make an additional stop to buy cheap film at a discount store. Any film stock left over from a job will last almost indefinitely if kept in a freezer (but it must warm up to room temperature before being used).

Negative film for 35mm cameras is also available in many speeds, with the most common ASAs being 100, 200, 400, and 1000. The finest picture quality can be obtained with 100 ASA film, but it is the least sensitive and is not suitable for lower-light situations. A good compromise is 200 ASA film because it will work in many more low-light situations while still offering attractive grain and contrast. Faster 400 and 1000 speeds are excellent for low-light shooting, but the picture quality tends to stray from what most professionals want. Several rolls of the fast film should be kept on hand for special very-low-light situations—e.g., night shots—but the majority of location stills should be shot on 200 ASA stock. Finally, slide film is not appropriate for location scouting because prints are so much more convenient to view.

SPECIAL PHOTO TECHNIQUES FOR SCOUTING

Producers and directors do not look for "arty" photos when they send a scout out on an assignment. They want clear, realistic documentation of a site. Therefore, special lighting effects, lenses, filters, and odd angles should be saved for other, more personal work.

This is why the basic 50mm lens is preferred for scouting. Most important, the 50mm lens does not introduce any distortion into a photograph. It "sees" a scene in a familiar way—with the same perspective as the human eye. A wider-angle lens (less than 50mm) "squeezes" more into a frame—creating a greater perspective. A longer lens (more than 50mm) magnifies a scene, making objects look closer—or giving them less perspective. This lack of distortion with a 50mm lens provides a realistic representation of the spatial relationships in the photographic frame.

A wide-angle lens will make small rooms seem larger by exaggerating the perspective lines (see Figure 3.1). On the other hand, a long lens will make rooms look smaller and distances shorter. These effects can mislead someone viewing the resulting photograph because, often, the distortion is not readily apparent. Thus, the viewer may be unpleasantly surprised to discover that a room that looked in a photograph as if it measured a comfortable 20 feet × 20 feet in reality measures only a tight 10 feet × 10 feet.

Sometimes, a wide-angle lens is required because the comparatively narrow field of view of a 50mm lens simply cannot capture either important details or the general feel of a small room. Small kitchens, bedrooms, basements, or attics are all good examples of this situation. But be aware that the wide-angle lens makes a room appear larger than it actually is. Whenever scouts use anything other than a 50mm lens, they should clearly note the lens size on the photo so that the viewer can correctly interpret the perspective shown.

THE PHOTO FLASH

Indoor flash photography is best kept to a minimum. First of all, the harsh, glaring look of flash photography can make any room appear ugly. Flashes create sharp shadows and can easily overexpose a photograph. Scouts can have one good location after another rejected merely because someone does not like the photographic quality of stills taken with a flash.

It is not a bad idea to let a location's natural lighting be the dominant light source, with bright windows shining out in a darkish room or color temperatures of existing lamps and chandeliers mixing with outside light. This creates a nicely textured, natural look that many directors of photography are seeking anyway. When necessary, scouts should use the very fast but grainy film stocks that will photograph even in candlelight, especially if the only alternative is a washed-out flash shot. It is important for scouts to show sensitivity to the photographic potential of a site, so again, they should undertake

Taken with a
35mm lens.

Taken with a
50mm lens.

Figure 3.1   Two views showing how a wider lens reveals more of a room. The photographer stood in the same position for both shots.

some serious practice to gain confidence in the limits of film stocks, cameras, and lenses.

On many occasions, an on-camera flash is definitely required to get an acceptable shot, but pains should be taken to use the flash in bounce mode whenever possible. The bounce mode diffuses the light, reduces shadows, and results in a more pleasing photograph. Not every flash unit has a bounce or "indirect" mode, but better models offer that option. Scouts should be sure that their flash attachment has it and that they know how to use it. Finally, cheaper flash units can have a frustratingly long recharge time between firings. The better models recharge almost instantly and are better suited to the quick shooting style needed by professionals.

THE PANORAMIC PHOTO SEQUENCE

Most rooms or sites will be too large to fit into a single photo taken with a 50mm lens. For example, a city block of row houses will have a much wider horizontal vista than can be captured with a 50mm lens. A wider-angle lens is one solution, but again, it is best to avoid the false perspective that such a lens can create.

The preferable solution is to take a panoramic sequence of shots. A panoramic sequence is produced by dividing a site into imaginary horizontal sections and then taking one shot of the far-left edge of the site, panning the camera an inch or so to the right to take a shot of the next section, and so forth (see Figure 3.2). This process is repeated until the entire subject has been photographed, section by section. Some sites will require three to four individual shots to complete a panorama. After the prints have been retrieved from the lab, the shots are assembled, creating the actual panorama.

When shooting, care must be taken not to tilt the camera up or down, which interrupts the horizontal lines. Also, the camera must not be panned so far to the right that a section of the site is skipped. To avoid this problem, a certain amount of overlap should be included in every segment. With each shot taken, the photographer must make a mental note of an object of reference (e.g., a fire hydrant, bush, tree, doorway, or car) on the right edge of the camera's viewfinder and, for the next shot, be sure that the same object of reference is seen in the left edge of the camera's viewfinder. This technique ensures that each shot has the necessary overlap, which will then be trimmed when the panorama is assembled.

Assembling the Panorama

When photographs are returned from the lab, they will probably not be in the order in which they were taken. This presents a number of problems in identifying any particular shot. Assembling a panorama can be tricky, somewhat like piecing together a jigsaw puzzle, because individual photos may have no memorable features. The scout may shoot dozens of locations in a day, and after a while, the images begin to blur together. For example, a scout who was supposed to have been photographing a panorama of houses in a city block could easily be puzzled by the presence of one shot in the panorama that shows a portion of a street intersection containing no houses at all.

If the scout needs to reshoot a panoramic sequence, it should be shot from a slightly different vantage point, so that when the prints come back from the lab, the segments of the two panoramas do not get mixed up. Trying to match slightly different views of panoramas that may each include five or six segments can be very confusing. Still-photo prints have no reference code to help the scout determine their order, so he or she can only rely on memory, and it is best not to muddle the work with lots of choices. Although it sometimes helps to refer back to the negatives, which do have reference codes, color negatives are not so easy to view.

The best way to sort panoramas, or any of the dozens of photos that might have been taken in a day's shoot, is for the scout to go through them as soon as possible after they have been retrieved from the lab, when his or her memory of the locations is fresh. In no time at all, the places seen and shots taken will blend together, and the scout will be faced with the daunting challenge of trying to remember what was shot where. A few notes written in a notebook on location (for example, "Red barn panorama, Smith Farm, corner of Rt. 128 & Valley Road") will also provide the scout with a great deal of help in sorting through the photos.

Once the panorama shots have been identified, they should be laid out on a table, in order, from left to right (see Figure 3.3). If attention was paid to the reference objects, there will be enough overlap in each photo, and no segment of a scene will be missing (see Figure 3.4). When the photos are matched, they are slid under each other until they become one long, apparently seamless photograph, which forms an impressive, comprehensive image.

Figure 3.2 How to shoot a panorama with a still camera. [Drawing by David Wilgus.]

Figure 3.3 Shots from a panorama spread out on a table.

Figure 3.4 Shots from a panorama laid out in a line.

Figure 3.5 Completed panorama.

Joining the photos requires a bit of both horizontal and vertical maneuvering. Any slight up-and-down tilting of the camera when the photos were taken will be evident at this point, and the photos in which this occurred will have more room at the top or bottom, depending on the amount of tilt. There should be no more than a quarter- to a half-inch difference, and if there is, more care must be taken to make steadier camera pans while shooting. With practice, the scout can improve on the alignment. The best way to minimize alignment problems when shooting is for the scout to be keenly aware of visual cues on the bottom of the viewfinder and take the time to match them from shot to shot.

Trimming the Panorama

After the panorama photos have been matched, they need to be taped so that they will stay in place. Initially, small pieces of slightly tacky adhesive tape can be placed on the front of the photos to join each seam. This tape is only temporary. When all the shots are joined this way, the entire panorama is turned over, and each back seam is completely and securely taped from top to bottom. Then the panorama is turned front side up again, and the pieces of "temporary" tape are removed from the glossy faces of the photographs. The top and bottom edges can be trimmed with scissors to compensate for any unevenness caused by vertical mismatching. With care and some practice, a good panoramic composition can be achieved (see Figure 3.5).

Solving Problems with the Panorama

Aside from composition and horizontal/vertical matching problems, there are several other pitfalls to be avoided when shooting panoramas.

First, there may be gross variations in color, exposure level, or focus between adjacent photos. These variations, which are usually caused by automatic cameras reacting to the changes in light or focus that might accompany each angle change, can ruin the panorama's seamless appearance. In settings containing great variations in light—for example, bright sky in one shot and a dark building in an adjacent shot—care should be taken to use only the manual exposure mode and then adjust the f-stop to achieve a single balanced exposure. As for autofocus, a foreground object such as a telephone pole or tree branch could throw the desired background out of focus and ruin a sequence.

Second, the optical distortion characteristics of wide-angle lenses result in visible distortion at the edges of each frame, which makes it impossible to match panoramic sequences shot with them.

And finally, labs, particularly one-hour photo processors, will often produce prints with excessive color and exposure variations from one shot to another. This is a problem, especially if there are big differences between lighter and darker subjects from shot to shot. Most one-hour processors use an automatic exposure mode, which will undo a photographer's careful exposure calculations. Although labs will generally redo poorly matched shots and make the required corrections, that takes time.

It is best to establish a relationship with a lab that understands the need for consistency between shots and will make an effort to achieve it. A good rule is to specify to the lab that all the photos be printed from the negatives at exactly the same exposure setting and not according to the autoexposure mode of the processor. Of course, the bottom line is that obtaining the best result from a lab depends primarily on correctly exposing the original negative, which means taking care to get the exposure right at the time the photo is taken.

MOUNTING THE PHOTOS

The favorite procedure for mounting location photos is to tape them inside legal-size (14-inch) file folders. Each individual photo or panoramic sequence must be carefully secured to the folder with clean, transparent tape (see Figure 3.6).

OLDER HOMES

120 Poplar St.
Partly cloudy 10 AM
Camera looking east

111 Oak Ave.
Partly cloudy 11 AM
Camera looking east

422 Wolfe St.
Sunny 9 AM
Camera looking west

818 South St.
Sunny 10 AM
Camera looking west

Figure 3.6 Location photos mounted in a presentation folder.

The stiffness of the folder stock provides good support for the photos and protects them from dirt, scratches, creases, or any other damage due to shipping. The folders also are helpful in organizing the large number of stills that are usually taken in a scouting assignment. The folders can be handled and passed around at meetings without the stills slipping out of order, falling behind a desk, or getting lost in an endless number of ways. The folders can be filed in a cabinet as well, with their index tabs handily identifying the contents for quick future reference. And the important information that must accompany each photo (discussed in the next section) can easily be written on the folders, beneath or beside the photos.

In short, folders are a good way to organize and present stills, and their use is standard with nearly all production companies.

DOCUMENTING THE LOCATION PHOTOS

In addition to the photographs themselves, there is certain important information that directors—and particularly directors of photography—will require about each exterior site to help them judge the quality and type of sunlight that falls there. The three most important items of information, which the scout must note at the moment of taking each photograph, are:

1. *The current weather and cloud cover, if any*: Weather is important because the cloud cover, or lack thereof, is an important factor in how well a site will photograph. Noting whether the sky is fully overcast, sunny, lightly cloudy, or foggy will help the viewer understand the look of the photo, because the sky may not appear in many photos. Sometimes, stills must be taken during a rain shower, and because it is nearly impossible to see raindrops in a photo, the gray haze that rain produces in a photographic image should be explained.

2. *The time of day when the shot was taken*: Time of day is important because, as the sun moves across the sky, buildings, trees, and other large objects cast various types of shadows that the director of photography must consider.

3. *The compass direction in which the camera is pointing*: Location scouts should always have a handheld compass and use it to note the direction the camera is pointing. This will enable the director of photography to consider how sunlight will fall on the site as the sun moves through the sky during the day.

Each of these items of information should be written in a notebook or log, then transferred to the back of each photograph when it has been retrieved from the photo lab. The information also should be written next to the photo when it is mounted in the file folder (see Figure 3.7).

The third factor noted here warrants further consideration because the way sunlight falls on a site greatly influences the scheduling of a production and the sort of lighting equipment it requires. In the Northern Hemisphere, direct sunlight shines from the south. Therefore, a building facing dead north will never receive direct sunlight. It will be lit with an even, diffused light all day long.

South-facing buildings are subject to the harshest sunlight, which also creates constantly moving shadows. An immense amount of lighting effort is therefore required to counteract the unreliability of natural sunlight. (Sunlight is undependable primarily because clouds may or may not block it and secondarily because the sun moves.) East-facing buildings will receive bright morning light and then indirect afternoon light, which can completely change their appearance. Exactly the opposite occurs with west-facing buildings: They will be in shadow when the sun rises but will be brightly lit all afternoon if there are no clouds.

Generally, a north-facing building is preferred because the sunlight will be more even and predictable. The director of photography can use just a few lighting fixtures to model the scene and have precise control over the quality of light. On the other

422 Wolfe St.

Sunny 9 AM

Camera looking west

Figure 3.7 Location photo with time of day, weather, and compass direction noted.

hand, sometimes a south-facing building is requested. Bright, direct sunshine will make any scene look sharper and let the colors sing, and some directors love that quality of light. Their scene may be short enough (or their budget large enough) so that they can live with the risks of using full sunlight.

All these factors are usually as important in judging a site as its overall look and character. Particularly in films and television, if a scene will require shooting for an entire day or even several days at the same location, the ambient light must be consistent for the production to move at the most efficient pace. From a producer's point of view, if lighting a site becomes a major undertaking, that site—no matter how perfect its look—may be passed up in favor of one that poses fewer lighting problems. Such are the disagreements the creative and administrative departments can have, and the location scout must be aware of these potential problems.

VIDEOTAPE TECHNIQUES

Videotaping is becoming an increasingly popular method of documenting a site. It has both a number of advantages over stills and a number of disadvantages.

Video's most obvious advantage, especially for film and television scouting, is that it most closely matches the capabilities of the motion picture camera. Large sites can be panned across, and tall buildings can be panned up and down—in a virtual rehearsal of scripted shots. Even the most basic video camera will offer the more familiar frame ratio of professional motion picture equipment and sometimes more comparable color reproduction than a still photo. Video's sound-recording capability allows scouts to provide simultaneous commentary, enabling them to describe many more details than they would normally have time to write in a notebook.

The favorite video tool of most scouts is the 8mm camcorder or the more expensive (but higher-quality) high-band 8mm camcorder because of its tiny size. Hardly larger than the palm of the hand, it can be easily carried up a ladder, aimed over a ledge, pointed out the window of a moving car, or held on the prow of a speedboat. Tiny 8mm cassettes can be popped into an air-express overnight letter and viewed a continent away in just a few hours. The scouting footage can even be edited into a rough version of a TV spot. This wonderful portability, combined with the motion and sound capabilities, has led many production companies to nearly abandon 35mm stills as a scouting tool in favor of the 8mm camcorder.

Although VHS camcorders are occasionally used as scouting tools, the full-size units are simply too bulky, in comparison with the 8mm units, to make them very popular. Although the compact VHS-C-type camcorders rival the 8mm units in size, if scouts are going to spend the money on a camcorder, they might as well spend it on an even more flexible and lightweight 8mm unit.

Video's primary drawback, and perhaps its only major disadvantage, is that it requires a playback system for viewing. Playback units for 8mm cassettes are still scarce. Furthermore, the units cannot be easily passed around an office or a meeting room, unless one of the even rarer handheld 8mm players with a built-in viewing screen is available. Of course, any television set can be used as a viewer, with the camera serving as the playback unit, so this is not really such a terrible limitation.

Another drawback is that duplicating video requires even more hardware and time—and results in a noticeable degradation of the image. Compared with stills, which can be copied half a dozen times at the lab or even photocopied and faxed at any office, copying and sharing videos is a much more unwieldy process.

The great advantage of paper print photos is that twenty of them can be spread across a tabletop at once and easily compared, grouped, and pulled aside. Twenty sites can be evaluated at a glance, without rewinding or fast-forwarding a tape. Electronic media still have a very limited, linear accessibility, which restricts the ease with which they can be manipulated. Future video units will undoubtedly have the ability to display multiple moving images simultaneously—but that technology, at an affordable price, is years away.

Although it is not necessary in every case, the ideal situation is to have both 8mm video and 35mm stills available as options. Some scouting assignments are perfect for video, and others demand the flexibility of stills. Some might think that using both methods is overkill, and it is definitely more expensive; however, it is best to be prepared for both, be proficient at both, and have both available for any scouting situation.

Location Suitability 4

CLEARANCES, PERMISSIONS, AND ACCESSIBILITY

As noted in Chapter 1, although appearance is 75 percent or more of what determines a location's suitability, there are many additional issues that scouts must address—and these issues have to be dealt with at the time the location is first scouted. Scouts often discover locations while driving by a site, without any initial contact with the owner of the property. But the scouts cannot simply take a snapshot and drive away thinking they have a good possibility. The owner must be contacted and needs to grant at least tentative permission before a site can be counted as a good potential location.

The easiest way to obtain permission to use a location is to find the owner and simply ask whether she or he would be interested in having the property used for a shoot. Private residences, businesses, and institutions require different approaches because each of them has its own set of problems. Generally, a shoot in a private home will affect far fewer people than a shoot at a business or some other site that is more open to the public. The more people affected by a shoot, the more problems there will be in obtaining permission.

APPROACHING PRIVATE RESIDENCES

When scouts approach a prospective location that is a private residence, they usually make the first contact by knocking on the front door and introducing themselves. Ideally, they will find someone working outside in the yard or on a car. When people are outside their houses, they tend to be more approachable, less on guard and suspicious. The response to the scouts' inquiry will vary greatly, affected by factors such as region of the country, economic level, and size of the community.

It is important for scouts to look and act like responsible professionals when seeking permission to use a stranger's home. Good locations are always hard to find, and a useful rule of thumb for scouts to remember is that a production needs a location more than a location needs a production, so a dash of high-class sales technique is necessary to obtain permission to use any location where it is obvious that the owner cares about the property.

Scouts should dress well, be sure their hair is neat, and have a friendly smile. A crisp, clean business card is essential and makes any homeowner feel more comfortable. A camera hanging from a strap around the scout's neck, along with a briefcase or clipboard in hand, will help to complete the expected picture of a professional media type.

Most people are extremely suspicious of *any* stranger knocking on their door because, usually, a stranger either bears bad news or is trying to sell something that people do not want. It is definitely *not* advisable to knock on strangers' doors after dark. Most people will be skeptical about the idea that someone from something so remote from their daily lives as a production company would suddenly appear at their door. Scouts must expect this attitude and be prepared to overcome it quickly. Scouts might have only a few seconds in which to gain the trust of the homeowner before he or she shuts the door; they need to be thoroughly prepared to put their best foot forward.

Beyond making a good appearance, scouts should open with a line like, "Hello, my name is Evan Casey, and I work for Lansing Productions, which will be making a TV commercial for AT&T in two weeks. We need to find a large, nice-looking home in the neighborhood to appear in the commercial, and I think your house would be a good possibility. If you're interested and your house is selected, you would be paid a location fee by our company." That speech will either lead to some questions or produce a terse "Not interested." From there, the scouts' success will depend on their ability to win the interest and enthusiasm of strangers.

To lend respectability to their request, it is advisable for scouts to mention any familiar, big-name company that may be involved such as AT&T, Pillsbury, or General Motors. People will not recognize the name of a local photographer or production company, but they will recognize the names of nationally known organizations (e.g., PBS or the big Hollywood studios) or the local TV stations. A friendly compliment about someone's home is always welcome, and mentioning a fee upfront will stir anyone's curiosity. Again, scouting for a location requires a talent for selling, and an upbeat, trustworthy pitch is the best way to succeed.

Dealing with Owners

It is important for scouts to deal with the owner of a property as soon as possible. They do not want to report that a location has been "cleared" for use unless they are certain it has. A family's teenage children might think it would be the coolest thing to have a heavy-metal music video shot on their front lawn, but their parents will likely have other ideas. Renters, delighted with the thought that a location fee would go into their pocket, could blithely give permission, which the actual owner might later retract.

Married people will always need to confer with their spouses, and housemates with housemates. People may need to consult their neighbors or community association in the case of longer-term or larger shoots. It is therefore rare for scouts to walk away from a location with a definite go-ahead after only the first look. People generally will have to discuss the proposition with someone or think about it for a little while.

People will often want to check the scouts' references as well. It is a good idea for scouts to notify the local film commission or chamber of commerce prior to commencing scouting on any project so that it may be given as a reference if one is requested. A letter of introduction from the film commission or any appropriate government agency is easy to obtain and helps make people less suspicious.

Again, the owner is the only one who can make a binding agreement granting permission to use a property, and scouts must make every effort to be sure they are dealing with the owner. The production company, director, and/or client will put some serious effort into considering each location possibility—including personally scouting it—and they need to know for sure, up front, whether they will be allowed to use it. There is little point in showing photos to the production team if the owner has denied permission from the outset.

Of course, there are exceptions. Sometimes, scouts are on a tight schedule, and it is simply impossible to get an answer in time. Or nobody may be home when they photograph a potential location. In such cases, scouts must clearly note that permission has not been obtained for that particular site. The worst thing to do is to set up a scouting meeting and present a dozen locations that have not been cleared. It is better to postpone the scouting meeting until at least some sort of positive response has been obtained from the owners.

Suspicious People and Problematic Homes

Location production, although fascinating to most people, is definitely a disruptive activity—one that is not right for everyone. The world is full of people who are cautious and/or suspicious, often with good reason. They may own rare and fragile antiques or have an expensively decorated home. Or the inside of their house may be a wreck, and they don't want anyone to see how they actually live! They may treasure their lawn and shrubs and would not want a fifty-person film crew turning the yard into a sea of mud on a rainy shoot day. They also might be nervous, nitpicky types, who keep their cabinets well stocked with household cleansers and are put off by the slightest hint of untidiness.

Instead of attempting to downplay the disruption a shoot would entail and convince overly suspicious owners, against their better judgment, that they should allow their home to be used, scouts will save a lot of headaches down the road if they just move along and find a more suitable property owned by someone more willing and able to deal with unfamiliar, disruptive activities.

Also, shooting in an expensively furnished home is a bit chancy because the production company is responsible for any damage that may occur. Crews can be rough on locations, and accidents do happen. Producers do not need the added risk of subjecting pricey decor to the vagaries of a fast-paced production. Rather than use a home furnished with delicate, irreplaceable objects and be liable for perhaps many thousands of dollars in damages, the production company would be better off using a home furnished with knock-offs that merely *look* expensive.

APPROACHING BUSINESSES AND INSTITUTIONS

Scouting for business and institutional locations requires a different approach from scouting for private homes. Typical nonresidential locations cover a wide range, including grocery stores, car dealerships, hospitals, courtrooms, restaurants, churches, banks, offices, schools, and so on. Although these types of locations are very different, they all share certain common problems. The main difficulty is that all of them exist to serve the public, and their doors must be open to the public on a regular schedule.

Since a location production can run really smoothly only if it can completely occupy a site, shooting in a business or an institution requires much more planning and usually greater expense than shooting in a private residence. A store can normally count on a fairly predictable income from one-time walk-in traffic. If it is closed to that traffic by a production, the owner will want to be compensated for the lost business. Many small-business owners are particularly worried that if they are closed at all during normal business hours, they could also lose regular customers who might get angry about the inconvenience or mistakenly think that the merchant has gone out of business.

Actually, except during the year-end holiday shopping season or on weekends, many businesses could close for a day without risking a great loss, but they will still worry about any lost income. The first question any business owner asks is whether customers will be able to shop normally during the shoot.

The answer depends on the circumstances and requirements of the particular shoot. For a big feature film, the production company may need to completely control one side of a city block or a small town's entire business district for a period of weeks or even months. For a TV spot or an industrial film, the company may just need to grab a shot or two outside a shop's front window. Many small entrepreneurs are sincerely interested in production. They may feel honored that their store has been selected as a location. They may see it as an interesting break from the usual humdrum routine of retail sales, or they may have some especially slow days when the extra cash from even a modest location fee would be welcome.

Large, high-volume businesses, such as discount warehouses, grocery chains, convenience stores, and department stores, will invariably regard production as a nuisance and a big liability, so unless they see a major publicity payoff, they generally are not interested unless the location fee is *very* high. At one time, the world-famous Plaza Hotel in New York charged $5,000 per hour to shoot on its front steps. Although this price may sound high, it seemed reasonable to an organized production company that could get its shot quickly and move on. The alternative would have been to spend as much as $50,000 to build the Plaza as a set.

The scouts' job is to get an idea of how receptive the owner of a particular business is to the idea of its being used as a location. There are so many reasons why an owner might be interested or disinterested that the response is almost impossible to predict. Every situation is different. If scouts don't ask, they will never know; so just as in approaching a homeowner, scouts should put on their most professional face and take the plunge.

It is important for scouts to remember that the majority of people are flattered when asked whether they would participate in a production. Unless they have been taken advantage of in the past, more often than not they will listen rather than turn scouts away immediately with a flat refusal. Scouts should be optimistic and suggest that it is indeed a privilege to be selected to appear in a motion picture production or a commercial photo.

Besides retail stores, the most difficult locations for which to obtain permission are businesses and institutions that see a lot of pedestrian traffic—for example, train stations, airports, banks, schools, courtrooms, and hospitals. Such sites have full schedules with very limited windows of availability—as well as substantial security concerns. They can only accommodate productions at odd hours or on weekends, if at all.

When scouts are looking for these sorts of locations, they should know what restrictions the producer has regarding the shooting hours. For plum locations, producers usually will adjust the shooting schedule to conform to the location's availability. It is not at all uncommon for a production to work at night or over a weekend to gain access to a busy location such as an airport, a shopping mall, or a grocery store.

The owners or managers of businesses and institutions usually are more concerned about liability than homeowners are. Their exposure is greater because they are open to the public. They have a sizable investment to protect. They are also more likely to be prey to a lawsuit should an accident occur. Legitimate production companies have substantial insurance policies as well as legal contracts stipulating that the production companies assume all liability. Although these provisions will satisfy many less paranoid business owners, there will always be some who are put off by their fear of increased liability.

The most difficult businesses for scouts to deal with are large operations with many branches. They usually have remote bureaucracies that prohibit any activity unrelated to their making money as efficiently as possible. Obtaining permission can be a frustrating exercise in corporate buck-passing, assuming the companies pay any attention to the scouts' request at all. Small mom-and-pop entrepreneurs are much more likely to be intrigued by the idea of their premises being used as a location; they are more likely to appreciate a modest location fee; and because they own the place, they can make a quick decision.

Special Concerns at Small Retail Locations

A commercial site is any property that exists to make money for its owner—a convenience store, a gas station, a hotel, a record store, a supermarket, a shoe store, an art gallery, or a restaurant. Such businesses all depend on the public to "drop in" and spend their money. If they are closed, there is no way they can make any money, so when a production company is determining the fee it will offer, it must be prepared to make up for the projected loss.

On certain days, very busy stores can make many thousands of dollars in sales. Their profit margin (high or low) must also be considered, so sales volume alone cannot determine the location fee. (This sort of negotiation, however, is really the province of the location manager and is considered in more detail in Chapter 6.) For the scout's purposes, it is sufficient to note the "busyness" of a particular commercial enterprise. A small mom-and-pop country store will present fewer problems than a teeming suburban mall. A struggling antique store owner on a quiet street might be glad to close on a weekday for a very modest location fee.

Just because a business appears busy at a certain time on a certain day does not necessarily mean it would be impossible or hopelessly expensive to obtain permission to shoot there. Businesses are often closed on certain days of the week (for example, many stores are closed on Mondays). And there might be certain hours when business is so slow that the establishment does not open or the owner wouldn't mind closing. For example, many restaurants are not open for lunch or have slow days during the week, and some stores are only busy in the afternoons or evenings.

It never hurts to ask because, in a single visit, a scout simply cannot determine all the restrictions on any given location. However, when looking for commercial locations, a scout should know, up front, whether the production company can be flexible regarding the days or times when it needs to shoot. For the majority of retail locations, this sort of flexibility is a must or else a prohibitively hefty location fee will be required.

Special Concerns at Business Office Locations

Business office locations differ from commercial sites in that they are much less dependent on casual "drop-in" traffic. They include banks, insurance companies, law offices, government offices, or any other type of office. It can be somewhat easier to secure permission to use such locations because their daily routines are fairly predictable, they are usually not crowded with people, and they can shift their operations without terrible inconvenience. They also have shorter hours of operation than a retail site (rarely beyond 5:00 P.M.).

This does not mean that it is simple to get permission to shoot in a business office. Many are filled with intently working people who cannot be disturbed by the comings and goings of a production crew. However, if the shoot will involve only a portion of a large office or only a single office within a suite, then moving a few people around for a day or so becomes a much less complicated proposition. There are many types of offices, each with its unique requirements, and once again, the only way for the scout to discover whether an office is available is to ask.

Special Concerns at Institutional Locations

Institutions include schools, hospitals, churches, museums, courtrooms, and other government sites such as police stations or jails. Institutions are somewhat like business offices, in that they do not depend on drop-in traffic and usually run on predictable schedules. They are a bit easier to deal with because they are generally large, so a section could be closed off to accommodate a production crew without causing huge inconvenience or loss of income. Many institutions will welcome a production crew paying a location fee because most are nonprofit and are happy to tap any source of income.

Certain especially busy or crowded facilities (e.g., department of motor vehicles offices, hospital operating rooms, or courtrooms) are in almost constant use and are employed for extremely important work that cannot be postponed. It is nearly impossible for the management of these facilities to accommodate any additional demands, including those that would be imposed by the presence of a production crew. Although obtaining permission to shoot in such locations is not out of the question, it does require unusual scheduling on the part of the production company and more than a little luck. In particular, it helps if the production company can provide the institution with enough advance notice so that it can find an unbooked time to reserve for the shoot.

On one particularly memorable occasion, I was seeking an 1800s-period courtroom for a week's worth of shooting on a PBS drama. Although I found a courtroom that had been perfectly restored, it was booked solid with trials for the next two years! After a little digging, I discovered that the judge who administered the courtroom needed to schedule some minor surgery that would keep him out of work for a week. He liked the subject of the production and offered to schedule his operation for the week that we needed the courtroom—a stroke of good luck.

One final note: determining fees for commercial, business, or institutional locations is quite difficult. There are so many different situations that it is impossible to employ a consistent strategy. When it comes to serious discussions regarding the price for using such locations, the scout needs to defer to the location manager because the negotiations can be quite drawn out. The scout's primary job is to present good possibilities, not signed, sealed, and delivered locations. (See Chapter 6 for a discussion of location fees from the location manager's point of view.)

CONSIDERING THE LOCALE

A major issue to consider when selecting any location is its surroundings. Although a location may look great and have a willing owner, its surroundings could present difficulties that must be taken into account. These difficulties, which are examined in the following subsections, primarily involve noise, accessibility, and neighbors.

Noise

Noise is not always a problem. It never is with still photography. But with film and TV, since dialogue and ambient sounds are carefully recorded with sensitive microphones, a location's general noise level is an important consideration. The worst sources of offensive sound are airports, large highways, and fire departments—each of which regularly, if not constantly, creates nearly deafening roars that can completely eliminate any possibility of recording good sound tracks.

Any location within a mile or two of an airport takeoff or landing flight path will have to suffer regular interruption by loud airplane engines. Each flyover will completely disrupt not just the sound quality but very likely the concentration of actors and crew as well. During certain periods of the day, even at airports that are only moderately busy, there can be a flyover every few minutes, ruining any hope of a successful production day. If a location is close to even a small airstrip, scouts must carefully check the landing and takeoff patterns and relay that information to the production company.

Any busy high-speed roadway generates a lot of sound from large diesel engines and the constant whine of tires on concrete. Because highway noise is a continuous drone, it may not be so immediately noticeable to the untrained ear, but sensitive recording equipment and the nature of film and video editing make extraneous noise a big problem. Furthermore, during morning and evening rush hours, road noise can be a hundred times louder than at midday, and that variation is important to note, particularly if the location is being scouted during low-traffic hours. It is always preferable, if not absolutely necessary, to select a location that is as far away from high-speed roadways as possible.

Fire stations are another obvious problem because, several times a day, fire engines—sometimes half a dozen at once—will roar out of them with barely muffled diesel engines, air horns blasting, and sirens screaming. Volunteer fire stations are even worse because they will blare their huge rooftop warning sirens for several minutes in addition to all the other noise that inevitably follows. Busy urban fire stations can send out noisy vehicles several times an hour. It is good practice for scouts to check a potential neighborhood for nearby fire stations and ask the commanders about their average activity level.

There are other "noise generators" too, such as churches with Westminster bells that chime every fifteen minutes, hospitals with frequent ambulance service, police stations, factories, lawn mowers, construction projects, and a host of others that scouts will all too soon discover—from marching band practice fields and dog kennels to skeet-shooting ranges. Most people are unaffected by these sorts of sounds in normal daily activity, but when someone puts on a pair of headphones and concentrates on recording dramatic dialogue, they become all too intrusive.

Noisy situations are not hopeless. The noise can be dealt with, or temporarily suspended, but it must always be a concern. Scouts only need to note the most obvious problems, but it does no harm for them to have a general awareness of conditions in the neighborhood. It is the location manager who needs to ferret out the hidden problems and deal with them once a location becomes a prime candidate. Location managers have more time to attend to such things than scouts do.

Exterior Accessibility

Accessibility includes such mundane but critical factors as parking space, stairs, road size and quality, height clearances, and staging areas. In a feature film or TV production, involving a sizable cast and crew and numerous large equipment trucks, accessibility is an important consideration. A beautiful house on a cute island that can only be reached by barge presents nearly impossible obstacles to a big production crew. Likewise, a home that has only two parking spaces and is situated on a narrow mountain road would be an inappropriate choice.

Also, most producers want locations to be less than an hour's drive from their home base. Not only are long drives at the beginning and end of the day tiring for everyone, but professional crews charge for travel time, sometimes at overtime rates, which is especially hard on a production company's pocketbook. Hence, long drives are a serious drawback for any location.

The quality of roads must be considered. Most production companies would think twice about shooting in a house on a low-lying peninsula whose only access road could be flooded or turned into a mud hole in a light rain. The effects of snow and ice must be weighed. Some driveways may not be wide enough for large equipment trucks. A beautiful mountain meadow cannot be used if it is only reachable via a steep, rocky footpath.

There are tunnels and parking structures whose ceiling heights can only accommodate passenger vehicles. There are old country bridges that are not strong enough to hold the weight of equipment trucks. There are many roads on which commercial vehicles are restricted. Finally, there are sites that simply lack adequate parking space for all the production vehicles, though this problem sometimes can be solved with some sort of shuttle arrangement. No matter what the situation, a scout needs to be aware of all these details and note whether any exterior access problems will seriously restrict shooting options.

Interior Accessibility

If the shooting site is a part of a larger location—for example, one room in a big house—the scout needs to consider accessibility to the selected area of the location. Long or numerous flights of stairs are taboo for most productions.

For example, an 1890s-period apartment on the sixth floor of an older apartment building without an elevator might look perfect; plenty of parking might be available; and permission might be easily obtained. However, the work required to hand-carry all the necessary lighting, camera, and sound equipment up to, and down from, such a location could make it too difficult to use, especially if it were needed only for a short scene. Moving equipment would involve many hours of extra labor costing many thousands of dollars. It would be much better to take the time to look further for a ground-floor apartment, especially if the scout wants to remain on friendly terms with the crew.

It is important for scouts to understand that a location is not just that portion of a site that will appear on camera. All productions (film and TV, in particular) need a number of sheltered staging and support areas—"backstage" areas. These include rooms in which lighting and camera equipment can be assembled and prepared, changing areas for actors, makeup and wardrobe areas, spaces where a caterer can set up and cast and crew can eat, and "green room" areas for talent and crew who are standing by.

Because heavy equipment must be carried in and out, some of the areas could be subject to fairly heavy wear and tear, so an unfinished basement or a garage is a plus. Dining areas can become pretty messy, given the inevitable spills, so an appropriate space must be available for eating too. Thus, if the script calls for a "living room," the production company will actually need a location that also allows access to a basement and as many as four other rooms in order to accommodate even a moderate production. A surprising amount of space is required, the reasons for which are detailed in Chapter 7.

Golden Rules for Location Accessibility

When considering both exterior and interior accessibility, scouts should be guided by the following rules:

- A location needs plenty of *close* parking for cast, crew, and equipment trucks. The parking area must be large enough so that it cannot become congested with cars and trucks that are either blocked in or have no turn-around space. A location must also be secure from the threat of theft or vandalism. Crews and actors can be dismissed at very odd hours in unfamiliar areas, so the personal safety of individuals walking to a dark, distant parking area must be considered. This often means hiring a security guard just to watch over the parking area.
- If a location is not on the ground floor, it should have elevator access. If it is higher than the second floor, it *must* have elevator access. Few locations are worth

hand-carrying the required tons of production equipment up more than two flights of stairs.

- Any time-of-day restrictions on access must be noted—for example, some buildings are unavailable on weekends, or some sites are only available on certain days of the week (hospital operating rooms, courtrooms, boardrooms). Some buildings are only open during normal business hours, and special arrangements must be made for early production calls or late working days.
- The roads leading to a location must be accessible to both passenger cars and large trucks in all types of weather.
- A location needs to be close to the base camp, which is discussed in detail in Chapter 7.
- There must be adequate support and staging areas to accommodate the "backstage" activities of a production crew.
- A location must satisfy basic safety requirements—have structurally sound floors, ceilings, and walls; have adequate emergency exits; and present no obvious hazards.

Neighbors

On any location, dealing with neighbors is a major concern. Again, by its nature, production is, to varying degrees, a disruptive activity. Although neighbors may not be paid a fee by the production company, they are still affected by the production and must be able to coexist with it, whether for several hours or several months. Neighbors include people living close to the location and businesses situated near the location, as well as people just passing by the location on a public road or sidewalk. A blocked road can actually cause more difficulties for commuters than for the people who live in a neighborhood, and inconvenienced commuters can be quite vindictive, so their needs must be considered too.

Although it is impossible during a scout to definitively gauge how a community will react to a production, scouts can usually get a pretty good idea. Homeowners whose house is being considered as a location must be asked about their relationship with their neighbors and what impact they believe a production might have on the neighbors. Most people are open-minded and curious enough to try almost anything once, including having their home or neighborhood used as a location, so scouts can usually be pretty optimistic about neighbor acceptance. But there is always the neighborhood crank to consider.

Some people have had bad experiences with production companies that were too disruptive, broke promises, or damaged something without fixing it. For most shoots, consideration must be given to how the presence of many people, cars, trucks, bright lights, and so on will affect the everyday activities of neighbors. Trash collection, mail and other deliveries, school buses, shopping, and work commute schedules can all be disrupted by a production. Although only certain inflexible individuals will be sensitive enough to resent even the slightest change in their fixed routines, most people will be quick to resent gross intrusions in their lives—and they should.

Some people move to quiet housing developments and pay high taxes in order to be shielded from such commercial intrusions as location film or TV production; others see such activities as a fascinating diversion that they were lucky enough to have been able to watch close-up. The range of reactions is remarkable, and the scout/manager must be prepared to cope with them all.

Particularly in situations that involve closing streets and sidewalks, a production's relationship with the neighboring businesses is important. Business owners are always concerned about customers' daily access to their premises, and most would be upset if they had to close for a day, as would anyone who was forced to lose a day's pay. This issue, which is one of the most difficult challenges of location management, is examined more closely in Chapter 6.

At this point, however, it should be recognized that the production will affect the neighbors, and the scout must get a sense about the neighborhood's willingness to accommodate a production. For example, if a property owner says that a year ago a TV crew shot across the street for a month of nights and all the neighbors petitioned to throw them out, then the scout needs to put that in his or her notes.

THE LOCATION SCOUT FORM

Much of the information discussed in the preceding section can be recorded on a location scout form (see Figure 4.1), which is basically a checklist of the most important issues to consider during a scout. On a smaller production, this form could serve as the only information sheet needed; on a larger production, a longer, more detailed, customized checklist may be needed for each location.

In filling out each item on the location scout form, only a few key words are required to document the scouts' findings. For example, under "Parking," the notation "plenty, next door" would suffice; under "Comfort," the notation "six bathrooms in home" or "none, need honey wagon," would suffice.

Scouts should not hesitate to make whatever sort of checklist they need in order to convey as much information as they feel is required about a particular site to satisfy the demands of a particular production. Once the location has been chosen, the location manager may add even more information regarding certain points on the form. The scout should not be expected to know all the details, but it does no harm to assemble as much information as possible early on so that it will be available later.

A good location scout form will include at least the following items:

- *Script location*: This is the name of the location in the script, such as "a country gas station."
- *Actual location*: This is the real site scouted such as "Leo's Country Store and Filling Station, 162 Evna Rd., Boring, Maryland 21171."

- *Contact*: This includes both the name and phone numbers of a contact person—usually, the owner; if not, then the person who can provide information about the site.
- *Light*: For interiors, are the existing (practical) lights tungsten, fluorescent, mercury vapor, or oddly colored? Can they be controlled? Are there large banks of windows/skylights that can be covered?
- *Sound*: Any notable sound problems—airport, construction, PA system, machinery, echoey rooms?
- *Power*: Is sufficient electric power available, or will a generator be needed?
- *Water*: Is there sufficient running water?
- *Holding*: Is there space for extras to rest and change in?
- *Staging*: Is there a room for preparing equipment?
- *Dressing*: Is there adequate space for changing clothes and for doing makeup and hair? Are separate areas available for men and women? Are these areas secure? Do they contain enough tables and chairs?
- *Meals*: Are there restaurants nearby? Are they open during shooting hours? Is there a sheltered area where a caterer can set up, and is there room to set up tables and chairs at mealtimes?
- *Parking*: Is there enough, and is it nearby?
- *Comfort*: Are there usable rest rooms nearby for men and women?
- *Neighbors*: Any obviously unfriendly?
- *Access*: Are there any problems inside or outside (e.g., no elevator, lots of stairs)?
- *Pay phone*: How close is the pay phone, where is it, what is its number, and can it receive calls? Regular phone that can be used?
- *Fees*: Were they discussed? How much?
- *Trash*: Dumpster? Needs to be hauled away?
- *T&T* (meaning "transit and traffic"): Will road closures, detours, or special parking permits be needed?

- *Security*: Will guards be needed during shooting and while the crew is away?
- Police: Will police be needed to control traffic?
- Fire: Will there be any special effects that would require the fire department to stand by?
- Permit: Is a permit required?
- Miscellaneous: Are there any unique problems that should be noted, such as nasty neighbors, soggy ground, or inoperative air-conditioning?
- Directions: Written directions should be provided—for example, "Take I-77 to exit 33. Make a right at the first red light. Make a right onto Kingston Rd. It's the first driveway on the left."
- Diagram: This should include information about parking, support areas, compass direction, access doors, and camera positions, as well as a rough map to aid in providing directions.
- Notes: This should include any other miscellaneous information, such as "grass needs to be cut day before shoot" or "street lights need to be shut off on shoot night."

LOCATION SCOUT FORM

Production: _____

Script location: _____

Actual location: _____

Contact: _____
        (name)   phone (h)   phone (w)

••

Light	Permit
Sound	Stairs
Power	Elevators
Water	Access
Holding	Pay phone/Phone
Staging	Fees
Dressing	Trash
Meals	T&T
Parking	Security
Comfort	Police
Neighbors	Fire

Miscellaneous:

••

Directions/Diagram:

Notes:

Figure 4.1 Sample location scout form.

5

Presenting the Location
Possibilities

THE LOCATION MEETING

When all the initial contacts have been made, the photographs taken and mounted in file folders, the scout forms filled out, the owners of potential locations contacted and their tentative approval obtained, and the fees and costs determined to be within the budget, then the location scout must present all this information to the producer, director, and other department heads. This occurs at a special production meeting scheduled to discuss location possibilities. For a large production, this meeting can be a long, drawn-out affair, because dozens of locations must be considered. For a TV spot or still photo, involving only one location and with just a few possibilities to consider, the meeting could take only a few minutes.

Face-to-Face Location Meetings

When scouts are working for a local production company (either a company that is actually based in the area or one that has come into town for a long or short project), a face-to-face meeting is called. This meeting is usually intense, and scouts will be asked many questions. Any hesitant answers or incomplete information will be obvious to the representatives of the production company, the ad agency, and any clients, so scouts need to be especially well prepared.

The location meeting will cover a range of questions. The production team will mostly be concerned with creative issues such as: Can the location be altered in any way (e.g., repainted, doors changed, shrubbery removed)? What does the other side of the street look like (for reverse angles)? How does the sun fall on the building at various times of the day? Creative issues will be the focus because it is assumed that the scout would not have presented the photos as possibilities if the sites posed any serious technical or logistical problems.

The question of alteration is inevitable, since no location is perfect, and no director is ever satisfied unless his or her personal creative stamp can be affixed. As members of the creative team discuss how to make a location look more like what they want or need, there will be many questions about how far the production company can go to change a location or control its appearance. As part of the decision-making process, the scout will take these questions back to the owners for answers.

Psychology of the Location Meeting

The scout must realize that creative media types often are extremely opinionated and extremely self-confident. They feel that they are the leaders and that leaders must make decisions in order to justify their position (and high salaries). Many of these "creatives" actually have no clear idea about what they want and demand a multiple-choice menu of possibilities. They can then select from four or five options and congratulate themselves on their brilliance in having discovered the perfect location. It is, of course, the scout who has assembled the choices, but never mind that.

Experienced scouts and location managers know that the more choices there are, the happier the creatives will be. Scouts who have seen the locations in person also know that certain locations will have much better logistics than others. The goal is to have the creatives choose the most easily workable site— provided it has the correct look.

This is not always possible, but scouts/managers will be letting themselves in for big trouble if they show a director a location that has many logistical drawbacks like uncooperative neighbors, noisy highways, heavy traffic, and all the "unseen" location problems that must be avoided. Directors will stubbornly fall in love with unworkable sites, so if scouts do not want to deal with impossible logistical problems, they should discard the photos of difficult sites and keep searching until both the look and the logistics are right.

When presenting the photos, scouts should take care *not* to show the best photos first. No creative person wants to be accused of accepting the first thing shown to him or her. It is also good psychology to present a few photos of truly bad possibilities up front, to make later ones look better in comparison. This is not deceitful; rather, it demonstrates an understanding of how the process works. Although it is a timeworn cliché, scouts should always save the best for last. Experienced scouts can spot a perfect location and can generally tell at first glance that it will be the final choice. There is likely to be much hemming and hawing among the creatives, often for days or weeks, but in the end, the scouts' first choice will usually be everyone's choice.

There can be many scout meetings, especially in larger productions. Creatives often will have scouts go out and keep looking for an elusive perfect location, even up to the night before the scheduled shoot. This sort of situation is immensely stressful on scouts/managers. The best way to avoid it is to steer the creative team into making a decision. Scouts should display total confidence at the location meeting. They should act as if they had left no stone unturned in their search for the director's perfect location. If scouts meekly whimper that perhaps they could have done better, they will lose the production team's confidence and will surely be sent out on a last-minute, panic-driven search. That is neither fun nor productive.

Generally, producers will be supportive of scouts because they are aware of the logistical headaches that can result from a poor choice of location. Directors, however, are sensitive to being steered, and good scouts must steer without being too obvious. The best strategy is for scouts to act totally noncommittal about the creative merits of a location but still present their photos and comments in a way that favors what they regard as the best location.

There are plenty of difficult directors who believe that being contrary is a mark of creativity and dismiss a perfectly good location only because they feel that an enthusiastic scout is trying to steer them. There is a quiet, skillful art to "selling" a location, and experience will show scouts the best psychological avenues to follow, depending on the particular type of creative team they are facing. It can be a stimulating challenge and reinforces the notion that scouts are important members of the creative team.

WORKING FOR OUT-OF-TOWN COMPANIES

If scouts are working on their home turf for an out-of-town company, all the "meetings" may take place by phone, with photos shipped via overnight express—a fairly common situation. If this is the case, then scouts must either make duplicate prints of the scouting photos for their own reference or at least make black-and-white photocopies of the mounted photos. Because the out-of-town production team will need to ask questions about the photographs, scouts must have an exact copy of the photos in order to discuss them quickly and easily while on the phone. It is also a good idea for scouts to number each of the photos before sending them to facilitate reference during phone conversations.

Time is of the essence in getting scouting photos to an out-of-town production company, so scouts must know the best methods of shipping from a particular area. Federal Express and other express messenger services have different cutoff times depending on the city and area of the country one is in. The offices that are open the latest are situated at or adjacent to the local airport, and 8:00 or 9:00 P.M. is generally the deadline. Attentive scouts will have this information and be sure that their schedule will permit them to get the photos to that office in time for next-morning delivery. For truly conscientious scouts, it is a good idea to find a one-hour photo lab near the airport depot for really last-minute runs.

Fax machines are being used more and more to send photos around the country quickly. They can save scouts a great deal of time. Production companies might need feedback within hours of their call, and the technology is there to deliver it. The main problem with faxes is that their detail is not very good, and they only transmit in black and white. The color of a location is an important consideration, so faxes are not acceptable in most situations. However, for some productions with killer deadlines, fax quality is all that is needed for initial scouting, and the fax is a wonderful tool when immediate feedback is required.

In the not too distant future, scouts probably will be able to transmit live color video via satellite to a production office 5,000 miles away and discuss the pros and cons of various location options with the producer over a simultaneous phone link. But for today, scouts still have to rush to meet the air-express deadline and be by their phone the next morning with notes in order, ready to answer a barrage of questions when the producer calls.

IN-PERSON LOCATION VISITS

When all the photos have been viewed, discussed, pondered, and narrowed down, it is time to actually take the production team to the location in person. Although the first in-person scout will usually reinforce the preferences that emerged during the scout meetings, it also will reveal any serious shortcomings of a site. Common disappointing discoveries include the following:

- The rooms in a location are too small to shoot in. If the scout used a wide-angle lens to photograph a room, then it will always be much smaller than it appears to be in the photos. Some rooms are simply too small to get camera, lighting, and sound equipment into without expensive demolition.
- The colors are wrong. When still photos are printed in a rush by a one-hour lab, their color can be very inaccurate, and the location's true colors may be unacceptable and unchangeable.
- The location is in lousy physical condition. A 5 × 7 still photo can hide many physical defects in a location, which become obvious on personal inspection and will be further magnified when the location is shot and presented on professional equipment. The site may require too much dressing to work in the scene.
- The location is in an inappropriate area—for example, reverse angles and wide shots will not work because styles or periods do not match.

These first in-person scouts will still primarily address only the creative aspects of the location. It is understood that scouts have considered the technical and logistical problems—parking, neighborhood, and noise—on their own prior to submitting the site as a possibility.

The creative team will want to see each location in person and may want to visit each site several times to compare and contrast—if it has the luxury of time. Hopefully, one location will finally be accepted as the team's favorite. But the team may reject all of them. If all the possibilities are rejected, and if there is time, the scout will have to go out and look some more, basically starting at ground zero. It is not terribly uncommon for the creative team to reconsider some of the sites that had been eliminated early in the scouting meetings. A lot of minds and concepts are changed following the in-person scout. That is when the decisions are really made.

This process will continue until the best location is found or the production company runs out of time or money. Eventually, a final choice is made, and at this point, the scout has effectively finished his or her work.

Skipping the In-Person Scout

If the production is small—such as a TV commercial, an industrial film, or a still-photo shoot—the production company often skips the in-person scout. The company may not have the luxury of time, or it may not have the money to pay a scout to take all the creatives to the site. In a small project, the location usually does not assume the importance that it does in a long drama or feature film. Particularly with many television commercials, a location may only be seen in a few frames, and the creative team can determine everything it needs to from the stills.

Out-of-town production companies are also less likely to conduct in-person scouts because of the added costs of transportation, lodging, and per diem. There is much more concern about time as well, and so approval is generally quicker.

Skipping the in-person scout can make the scout's job easier, because it eliminates the possibility of the creative team's discarding all the potential sites—and forcing the scout to start all over again. However, there is always the chance that when the members of the creative team arrive at the location on the shooting day, they may hate it. At that point, they may send the scout/location manager out to find a new site in a matter of minutes—a difficult situation, indeed!

If the production company dislikes a site that the creative team has not personally visited, then it is not the location scout's fault. In this situation, though, the scout needs to be *extra* careful not to have misrepresented or exaggerated something about the location that then causes it to be rejected. Such conduct is unprofessional and will cause the scout to be judged harshly for either misleading the team or doing sloppy work.

When a location is rejected on the shooting day, scouts need to swallow hard and carry on. Although it might seem to be a disaster, what usually creates this situation is that the director has spotted something next door or nearby that he or she feels is better. All scouts need to do is approach the new choice. If the owners say yes, then the scouts are heroes. If the owners say no, then at least the creative team got a quick answer with little agonizing, and the production will most likely go back to the original choice. Only three things in life are certain: death, taxes, and directors' changing their minds.

THE TECH SCOUT

The tech scout is the final scout before shooting. Prior to scheduling the tech scout, all the locations have been initially visited and photographed. There has been at least one meeting with the creative heads to discuss all the possible locations, and some of them may have been visited during in-person scouts. The creative heads have then decided on their favorite location. All approvals have been obtained, and there is no obvious obstacle to filming at the selected site. Barring a major disaster, there is no chance that a location will change during the tech scout.

The tech scout is primarily an informational tour of the location for the benefit of the various technical or craft department heads. The director, producer, director of photography, gaffer (lighting director), art director, and sound recordist usually attend the tech scout, which is led by the location manager. The scout is generally not required to attend the tech scout— unless he or she is also serving as the location manager.

TV Commercial Tech Scouts

Elaborate tech scouts are not required for the average TV commercial. Most often, this tech scout will be attended only by the producer or director and the director of photography; they have the background to determine how suitable a site is for all departments. They can judge lighting requirements, the set dressing needs, potential sound problems, and all the logistical problems (in cooperation with the scout/manager).

If they discover some potential problems, then they can determine whether any prep days will be needed by any other department head and make the necessary arrangements. On a TV commercial shoot, everyone is paid very well and by the hour, so producers do not want to have unnecessary personnel hanging around at great expense.

Particularly in the case of an out-of-town production company, the tech scout will be a quick affair. As advisable as it would be to have the head of each department inspect a location for potential problems, it would also be prohibitively expensive to bring them all in to view a location that will be used only for a one-day shoot. On a commercial, most major or minor location problems can be overcome because the site will not be occupied for very long and can be altered through all sorts of lighting techniques and set dressing.

TV commercial producers and directors have learned to be quite adept at making a location "work." First, they are on a fixed budget, and they do not have the luxury of being able to adjust a shooting schedule as longer productions can. Second, they have usually submitted a fixed bid to produce the commercial and do not want their own fussiness to cause an excessive financial burden for their company. They will bend over backward to convince a skeptical agency or client that even though the location may not be exactly what everyone had in mind, they will have no problem making it work.

Sometimes, there is no tech scout at all. Although this is quite rare, it does happen. If there is a killer production deadline or it is a very low budget shoot or the location simply is not very important, then the company may pull into town, "site unseen," and make a go of it. This approach can work, but not previewing a location at all has caused many people many headaches, and experienced professionals have learned not to trust an unseen location. Good scouts can foresee the majority of problems, and this is the best reason for hiring dedicated, experienced scouts, whose good taste and attention to detail can be trusted.

Feature Film Tech Scouts

Because feature films, television films, and other long-form dramatic productions involve many more elements than a TV commercial, they require much more attention in the tech scout. A feature film can have a staff of a hundred or more persons. It can involve dozens of vehicles. It can require many complex lighting setups, stunts, and special effects scenes. It can use dozens of different locations. TV movies will have shooting schedules of three to four weeks. Some big feature films have shooting schedules that span three to four months. These vast productions require careful scheduling. Some films will change location twice a day. Others will stay in one spot for weeks.

Given the precise scheduling demands of features, neither the technical crew nor the creative crew has much time, once the shooting starts, to go on location scouts. They are too busy shooting. Therefore, all locations need to be scouted in advance by the creative and technical department heads.

A feature film tech scout will always include the producer, director, assistant director, production manager, location scout/manager, script supervisor, transportation coordinator, art director and/or production designer, director of photography, gaffer, key grip, and sound mixer. It is not uncommon for the costume designer and even the makeup artist to visit a location to help them get a feel for the story's setting and how to make their work harmonize with it. Sometimes each department head's assistant will attend the tech scout so they can be aware of the situations and work out plans on the spot. Even production assistants may tag along to help prepare maps to the locations and become familiar with the logistics.

All these people create quite a crowd, so at least one if not two large passenger vans are required. Who sits in which van can be problematical, and it is a good idea to have walkie-talkies so the people in both vans can communicate with each other while traveling from location to location. During these drives, there will be plenty of discussion about what everyone has just seen, and it is frustrating for a director not to be able to ask a quick question of the sound mixer, who might end up riding in another van. One practical suggestion: A cooler full of drinks and some snacks will be appreciated by all and makes the tech scout a bit more pleasant.

And making it pleasant is quite an undertaking. A big tech scout will easily take at least one full day. It is invariably exhausting. Everyone scribbles notes on the assets and drawbacks of each site. Because ten or more locations might be visited during the course of the day, not much time is available to view each site and questions must be answered quickly. On a union film, a teamster will drive the van, but on most nonunion films, the location scout/manager is expected to drive. Who else knows the way to each site? It will be a hectic, difficult day for the scout/location manager.

Therefore, the day must be carefully scheduled. The tech scout includes all of the busiest, highest-paid personnel, and they do not appreciate their time being wasted. The day before the tech scout, location scouts must be sure that all their contacts will be ready and standing by at each location, according to a prearranged schedule. It is an excellent idea to have a cellular phone in the tech scout vehicle so that any last-minute changes can be handled smoothly.

A typed schedule should be prepared and distributed. Travel time needs to be figured accurately, and the routes from one location to another must be carefully mapped out. A quick lunch and possibly a dinner stop should be preplanned at a restaurant that can satisfy ten to fifteen picky, rushed eaters. Rest room and phone breaks must also be built into the schedule.

The tech scout, then, is the showpiece of location people. If they impress the crew with their organization and punctuality during the tech scout, they will make many friends. If they get lost, can't get into a location, or drive like fools, they will lose the confidence of the people who matter most. Regardless of what real backstage chaos they might be facing, members of the location department must appear cool, enthusiastic, and together—and have the answer to every question. A good tech scout will set the course for smooth sailing for the rest of the production.

$$6$$

The Work of the Location Manager

LOCATION SCOUT VERSUS LOCATION MANAGER

The line between location scout and manager becomes blurred as the start of shooting approaches. The location scout is the person who searches for the location. The location manager is the person who finalizes all the business arrangements with owners, neighbors, and local authorities. The location manager also oversees the relationship between the production crew and all nonproduction persons at the location during the shooting.

THE LOCATION DEPARTMENT STAFF

Location managers may have one or several scouts working for them and might spend most of their time on the phone and handling administrative tasks such as assessing location photos, making deals, and taking other department heads on short in-person scouts. The location scouts may simply be feeding photographs and scouting reports to the location manager, who organizes this material and presents it to the production team.

On very large productions, there will be a single location manager and probably more than one scout. More commonly, the location scout will ease into the role of the location manager as more and more of the sites he or she has found are locked in. The scout will then negotiate the deals and handle the necessary day-to-day logistics that are the province of the location manager.

On almost any feature film, the location manager will have a staff. His or her first deputy is the assistant location manager, who shares many of the administrative duties, both in the production office and out on location. When a production has many locations and a fluid schedule that changes due to bad weather, a slow director, casting difficulties, script revisions, and other common production problems, one person cannot handle all the duties of the location department. Many productions will add a location production assistant (location PA) to do much of the drudge work, such as drawing maps and cleaning up the location, which frees the location manager and his or her assistant to deal with more pressing concerns.

LOCATION FEES

A location fee is the main reason for anyone to consider allowing their property to be used as a production site. It is money paid to owners as compensation for a production company's temporary use of the property. It is basically a short-term rental fee, similar to a car rental or a vacation house rental at the beach. Being paid a hundred dollars just to have a few pictures taken of their house can seem like "free money," especially to those who have never seen a production crew working on location.

On the other hand, many people do not realize how much production companies are actually willing to pay for a location.

Surprisingly, some people caught up in the glamour of "show-biz" may not expect to be paid anything at all. They feel it is a compliment to have their house selected for a production and that it is a privilege to be able to watch the cast and crew up close. Once they experience the immense amount of work and disruption that location shooting involves, they often have second thoughts.

Given the substantial disruption that full-blown productions cause, it is always wise to assume that a reasonable location fee should be paid, particularly to individuals who have no reason to cooperate other than to earn some money. It is preferable to keep location agreements on a businesslike basis, since friendly deals (and friendships) can be strained to the breaking point by the surprising demands and disruptions of a production crew. It is almost universally true that experienced film, television, or still photography professionals would never let their home be used as a location unless they were paid a huge amount of money—and even then, perhaps not. That says a lot about what location owners can expect, and why getting some payment is nearly always advisable.

There are exceptions, however, under which owners may waive the location fee. Such exceptions frequently occur in the case of sites that are being used for a public service announcement or public television program. People understand that supporting a charity or some other worthy cause could extend to allowing their homes to be used as a location, so production companies making public service announcements for nonprofit organizations, such as Pets on Wheels and antidrug spots, rarely pay location fees.

Publicly Owned Locations

Government-owned sites or facilities often do not charge location fees. Various levels of government deliberately establish such policies as a marketing strategy to lure producers to their locale. Film commissions love to promote the fact that, in their area, no fees are charged for the use of any state or municipal sites, facilities, or services. And in many situations, this amounts to important savings for producers. The governments justify these freebies because they feel that the income generated through sales and income taxes, together with the overall economic stimulus and PR associated with multimillion-dollar productions, outweighs any income that might have been generated through location fees.

Certain popular government-owned properties—particularly airports or any facility dealing with mass transit—may charge a location fee. These locations are difficult to control, so the government incurs a big expense for the extra planning and security required to ensure that the public is protected and disruption of important schedules is minimized. Overtime charges for guards and the hassle of pulling supervisors away from their regular duties so that the shooting goes smoothly can be a major inconvenience to an airport or a similar facility, costing the government authority many thousands of real cash dollars. In such cases, the location fee generally just covers expenses and is not considered to be a "profit center" for the government. Furthermore, in airports and mass-transit facilities—with the public rushing to catch various trains, buses, and planes—there is great potential for frayed tempers and loud complaints, so government agencies will usually only want to deal with very organized companies in these situations.

Eventually, some local governments decide, after several (or many) experiences, that accommodating any production work for free may not be worth the taxpayers' money, and they start to charge fees and/or require expensive permits for everything. When complaints from the public keep coming in about a location, it is probably being overused. Local bureaucrats then conclude that financial incentives are no longer needed to lure producers to their area.

Obviously, the Los Angeles area falls in this category, but nearly every big U.S. city has some popular neighborhoods where severe restrictions have been imposed due to the volume of producers who wish to shoot in them. Cases in point include

Greenwich Village in New York City and Georgetown in Washington, D.C.

The Producer's Authorized Price

Because there is such a wide variation in both the suitability and proper amount of a location fee, it is important for the scout to determine what the producer wishes to pay. Some producers are generous; others will want to pay much less than the location owner's time and cooperation are worth. The scout only needs to know the approximate price range and then indicate the property owner's reaction in his or her report to the production company.

If the scout is authorized to offer $500 per day for a location and the location owner quickly accepts that as fair, then the fee is not a big issue for the scout. If the location owner states that $1,500 per day would make it more worthwhile, the scout should emphasize that the particular location is only a candidate and that price will be an important consideration in making the final choice.

Because production companies often find money in their budget for more expensive locations that may seem especially desirable to the creative team, scouts should not automatically dismiss any price request. They should make a careful note of the desired fee and relay that information to the production company while remaining cheerful and sympathetic in their dealings with the location owner. The producer, production manager, or location manager will have a much better idea of the production's financial, logistical, and creative needs and should handle the final price negotiations.

Pricing Residential Locations

Unfortunately, there are no standard prices for locations: everything is negotiable. As a rule of thumb, many production managers will allow about $1,000 per day for an average site. It is a nice round number that sounds attractive to a homeowner and will usually land any desirable site. Although that may seem like a lot of money, it is actually only a small percentage of virtually any professional production budget. It is also a fraction of what it would cost to build an appropriate set and shoot the scene in a studio.

Three issues must be taken into consideration in pricing a location: the uniqueness of the location, how long the production company will need to use the location, and the extent to which the crew will occupy the location. Let's start with the first of these factors—uniqueness. If the desired location is a simple bungalow that has hundreds of look-alikes, the fee might only be a few hundred dollars. The producer will not want to pay a high fee for a common location because, if a lot of choices are available, the company can probably find someone willing to accept a lower price. If, on the other hand, the desired location is a palatial estate with an indoor pool, a grand piano, and a gourmet kitchen, it has a higher value, and a higher fee should be offered.

It generally can be assumed that the more unique a location, or the more expensive the property, the higher the location fee will be. Also, the simple fact is that people with large, expensive homes are more sophisticated about money and realize their demands will probably be met if they negotiate persistently enough. A young couple struggling with a mortgage, car payments, and nursery school fees usually would be happy to accept even less than $1,000 a day.

The second main factor in pricing a location is how long a production will use it. Sometimes, a home is needed only for a few hours, as in a TV commercial. For some feature films, a home may be needed for several months or more. The longer a location is required, the more the owners will be inconvenienced, and the more compensation they will want. If a location is to be used on a long-term basis, the owners may even be relocated to a hotel for a period of time, and the cost will be picked up by the production company.

More often, the owners will simply coexist with the cast and crew. Being in the midst of a big production can be an adventure of sharing meals and rubbing shoulders with movie stars and moguls and can afford owners a front-row view of the filmmaking process. Sharing one's home with a working production crew can be a priceless or harrowing experience—and is generally a good measure of both.

For short-term occupations of just a day or so, the location fee is often based on an hourly rate. However, to price a site simply as a "day" can lead to misunderstandings if the owner thinks of a day as eight hours and the production company thinks of it as twenty-four hours. It is best to specify how many hours a flat location fee buys and also to establish a reasonable rate for overtime.

The most negative experiences with location shooting usually involve homeowners who have no idea how complicated a production can be. They may be stunned to discover that it takes dozens of people fourteen or more hours of intensive work to produce a thirty-second TV spot and can become angry if they feel they have not been adequately briefed or actually have been misled by a production company or scout.

The final factor in pricing a location is the extent to which the site will be occupied by a crew. In some cases, the production might need to occupy the entire home from attic to basement, and in other cases, only the front porch might be required. Even with exterior shots, however, owners must be prepared for the fact that people will have to come into the house. Electricity from inside might be needed, or production lighting units might have to be placed so they shine out of the windows. Special window curtains or other window treatments might have to be hung from the inside. Actors may need to enter or exit a house or deliver lines from windows. Even these simple activities can involve at least half a dozen technicians parading through a house (often in their muddy shoes), laying yards of dirty cable, moving furniture, changing curtains, and more.

Even if the script calls for only one room—for example, a living room—much more support space will be required, and that same home must provide it. This space requirement can include a makeup and wardrobe changing room. A bedroom or large bathroom is commonly used for this purpose because it provides access to water and is somewhat removed from the general hubbub.

The production company also will need a place very close to the shooting set to temporarily store equipment that is not being used at a particular moment. This is known as the "staging" area. All the technical departments—particularly the lighting, camera, and sound departments—need a staging area to prepare and store individual pieces of gear, accessories, or expendable supplies such as lighting gels, tape, and rope. Running in and out of a house for every one of the hundreds of little items that are required to shoot a scene would demand an immense amount of time and slow down the shoot. Basements, garages, or playrooms are good candidates to use for staging areas because they usually have the least delicate decor and, therefore, are less likely to be damaged when various heavy light, camera, and grip equipment is being prepped and moved in and out.

Because a crew will often occupy a location for up to fourteen hours a day, an area must be reserved for eating and snacking. For a small production, about fifteen people will have to be fed breakfast, lunch, and dinner by an on-site caterer. A snack and beverage table (also known as *crafts service*) must be set up for easy access all day long. This means that three or four 8-foot tables and a dozen or so folding chairs will be required, plus serving tables for the caterer.

Food and drink inevitably spill, and crew members will continually be coming and going to grab a cup of coffee or juice, so this eating area needs to be set up in a room that will not suffer from doubling as a snack bar. Again, a garage (heated in a cold climate) or basement is ideal. If the weather is good, this area can be set up on a large porch or patio or in the yard. A tent can be erected for longer occupations, but all concerned must realize that lots of foot traffic on a lawn will quickly ruin it, particularly in bad weather. Common sense and a little experience will often be the best guide, with the general rule being that the more equipment and people there will be in a given space, the more durable it must be.

Finally, actors, directors, and even producers may need a quiet place to meet, study, go over lines, make important phone calls, or simply rest. A den, a library, or even a child's bedroom can serve this purpose very well, and the production company should consider making arrangements to be able to use these quiet places.

As usual, when a group of people will be working on location, rest room facilities must be considered. Most homes will have at least two bathrooms, and many have more. The one that is farthest from the shooting activity should be chosen, simply because the noise of a flushing toilet has ruined many a great take, embarrassing the errant flusher and even led stressed directors to fisticuffs. The location manager needs to check this shared rest room regularly because it will get a lot of use, and a backed-up drain on a location creates a messy problem no one wants to deal with. I remember one shoot in London during which a producer accidentally broke the toilet in a location apartment. The resulting transatlantic efforts to fix the loo and pay the bill required hours of the Baltimore-based production office's time.

Sometimes, one home—even including its garage and porch—cannot provide all the support and shooting space needed. In these cases, a nearby support area is required. A church basement or neighbor's home can serve nicely. In fact, it is often beneficial to have the support areas in another nearby home or building to cut down on noise and traffic problems. The owners of these support areas are paid a fee for the use of their space as well, which must be added to the total real cost of any location.

Often, expensive location vehicles—such as mobile dressing rooms, wardrobe trailers, and "honey wagons"—will be used on larger productions, particularly feature films or television dramas. These completely self-contained units have their own water, rest rooms, and electric power plants. They eliminate the need for extensive support areas, except for extras' dressing and holding areas, but the scout must also realize that each unit is the size of a large tractor-trailer and up to four or five must be parked in close proximity to the location. Not only must parking space be found for these ungainly vehicles (which is no simple task), but a substantial parking fee might also be required. Furthermore, these transportation units are expensive to rent, and their drivers are well paid.

These costs, which must be added to the total expense of the site, can be a concern—especially in the case of smaller productions that are being shot on location in the first place in hopes of dodging high production expenses. It is almost always cheaper to use existing nearby facilities than bring in custom units.

When a home is large enough to completely accommodate the support requirements, this results in a substantial savings to the production company, and at least some of the savings should be passed on to the location owner as an increased location fee, which compensates the owner for the extra wear and activity to which his or her property will be subjected.

Basically, the more space a production company uses in a house, the more it should pay; conversely, if it is only grabbing a shot of the exterior, a lower fee should be negotiated. The *location services contract* (see Figure 6.1) is a handy checklist that can be attached to the location release. It details the support items—parking, phone, and holding areas—that the location's owner agrees to supply. It is particularly useful if a property is being employed for support but not being photographed and a photo release is not required.

Pricing Commercial, Institutional, or Business Locations

Locations that are open for business or provide any sort of service to the public involve a set of concerns that are quite different from those associated with residential locations. The daily routines and operations of a commercial site affect dozens, hundreds, or even thousands of people, and those people will

LOCATION SERVICES CONTRACT

Name of property: _____

Address: _____

Contact name: _____

Telephone: _____

Dates: _____

Hours: _____

Production company: _____

Production: _____

Services (yes or no):

_____ Extras holding	_____ Dumpster
_____ Extras changing	_____ Equipment staging
_____ Extras meals	_____ Water
_____ Crew meals	_____ Electric
_____ Auto parking	_____ Rest rooms
_____ Truck parking	_____ Telephone
_____ Makeup/Wardrobe	_____ Greenroom

•••

    I grant my permission for the above-named production company to use the above-named facility for the purposes checked above in connection with the filming of the above-named production.

    When finished, the production company will clean and restore the facility to the same condition as it was prior to its occupancy, except for usual and reasonable wear and tear.

    The production company agrees to pay for any extraordinary or increased utility charges (phone, electric, gas, water) incurred by the facility as a result of its occupancy of the facility, upon submission of documentation of these extraordinary charges by facility owner or manager.

_____   _____

For facility   For production company

_____   _____

Date   Date

Figure 6.1 Sample location services contract.

be affected by the presence of a busy production crew more than an individual homeowner or a single family would be.

More often than not, a production crew will require that a commercial site completely stop its normal operations, which can be an expensive proposition for the owner. How busy a particular location is will determine its price and the feasibility of using it. Of course, budget considerations here are very important. Producers know that a commercial site will cost more than a residence; however, they will be concerned about keeping the costs reasonable.

NEGOTIATING THE LOCATION FEE

Although it might be the scout who, with some initial guidance, first discusses the location fee, it is the location manager's job to finalize all pricing. In many cases, this is not a problem. If the requirements of a location are fairly simple, the owner amenable, and the logistics straightforward, then the authorized price that the scout initially quoted can be accepted by all, and a final agreement can be reached swiftly. For smaller productions, this process can involve nothing more than a handshake and the signing of a *location release* (discussed in detail later in the chapter).

In other cases, the process can involve serious, protracted negotiations guided by lawyers, with multipage contracts for each side. Some examples include shooting in a busy airport for several days, occupying an entire block in a city's downtown business district, using a large institution such as a college campus, or filming on a street in a residential suburban neighborhood for a long period of time.

As noted earlier, the primary factors in determining the location fee are: How much of the location will actually be needed, both for photography and for support; how seriously the production will disrupt the daily routines and/or business of the location owner; and how unique the location is. The combined importance of these three factors determines how much a location will cost.

Another consideration is the perceived value of a location to the owner for having his or her property appear in a production. In the case of a business that could use national exposure, the prospect of having the premises appear in a movie will often entice the owner to offer the site for free. In productions using resorts, cruise ships, theme parks, and so forth, some owners might even offer financial or other incentives to a production company to use their location because they perceive the promotional value to be so great. This is often the reason that government film commissions will offer all government-owned property at no cost: It can help generate national awareness of the (hopefully) positive aspects of an area and also boost civic pride.

Even in less commercialized circumstances, such as with a small local bar or house, the property owners can still perceive a shoot as highly desirable. The status value of having famous movie stars walking in one's backyard or the glamour of being associated with the cool, magical, mysterious world of production, if only for a day, has a definite attraction. There are plenty of tiny businesses with big signs boasting that scenes from a movie were filmed there. People selling their home have noted in the sales listing that movie stars once walked in the house. Nor does it matter that the films in question were long-forgotten flops.

Of course, all location managers will take advantage of these feelings as much as possible. Offering exposure, glamour, and status costs the production company absolutely nothing.

Standard Location Fees

There is actually no such thing as a standard location fee. The price of $1,000 per day was mentioned earlier, but that is strictly a function of time and place. Although that figure might be an average, most fees would be either higher or lower than that amount. This vagueness regarding pricing is due to the fact that most locations are used only once, so there is never any opportunity to set a consistent price. Despite the great boom in location production, the average owner of a home or business is unlikely to be approached even once about having his or her property used as a location. As a result, owners will have no personal frame of reference, and chances are, no one else they know will have had any experience with it either.

Furthermore, many people have no idea of the amount of money that goes into a TV, film, or still-photo shoot and would not want to appear greedy by asking for the many thousands of dollars it would cost to duplicate their home or business as a set. This is not so true in popular areas that are sophisticated about production, such as Beverly Hills, Greenwich Village in New York City, or Georgetown in Washington, D.C.; but in most of the country, each location must be negotiated on a case-by-case basis.

In the top one hundred or so U.S. population centers, there is generally some fairly active production community that handles local TV advertising needs, training videos, annual reports, and so on. In these areas, the successful companies may have established a local standard—for example, $250 per day for a home in Raleigh, North Carolina, which is much less than in the major production centers.

On a local level, and within certain local production companies, there can be some pricing standards. These standard prices can become very high, which is often why production companies leave the large, expensive production centers. By going to a less used area, they hope to save on location fees. In their mind, the owner of a house in Raleigh should not ask for a fee anywhere near as high as the owner of a house in New York City.

Ultimately, the most significant factor in determining the fee is how familiar an owner is with the range of fees paid for similar locations in his or her area or in other areas of the country. What will be regarded as an acceptable fee is also a function of the financial situation of the particular location owner. To some people, $300 is a welcome fee. To others, $10,000 might just begin to stir their interest. It all depends on uniqueness, size, duration, and of course, the "glamour factor."

Hidden Costs of a Location

A word of warning: The cheapest location may not be the most cost-effective in the long run. A location manager might haggle and cajole or even mislead a property owner to get such a low price that there will be trouble down the line. Many people will initially be lured by the glamour or the prospect of making a quick and easy $250. However, they will not appreciate a full production crew dragging equipment across their lawn, muddying their floors, scratching their walls, or disturbing their neighbors, and once they experience the extent of the disruption, they might regret their decision and become difficult.

It can be a great mistake to pressure someone into letting his or her location be used. Sometimes, due to the uniqueness of a location and the desperation of the location department, it cannot be helped. But where there are alternatives, it is always better to go with location owners who seem to be the most amenable and easygoing—the type of people who can put up with a high-energy production crew.

Owners can become frustrated and upset by the unexpected number of people and amount of equipment and the general hubbub of a production. If the shoot is going slowly, owners can become livid because they expected only a few hours of minor intrusion, not eighteen hours of having their home turned inside out. Some misled owners might demand that the production leave their premises immediately. The only solution to this situation might be for the production company to agree to a large increase in the location fee. Not only is this frowned on by the production office, but it is an embarrassment to the location manager as well because it reflects poor planning.

If location owners are paid a very low fee or no fee at all, then there is the danger of their not approaching the production in a serious manner. Paying a realistic fee lets owners know that a professional commitment has been established and that they must live up to their promises. It would be bad to have owners cancel their permission at the last minute because a friend asked them to go shopping, but it does happen. Unpaid owners might also make little effort to keep their promises regarding such details as leaving lights on in their home or moving their car from a driveway or informing their neighbors about the shoot. That can cost the production company a lot of wasted time and money. The higher the location fee, the more incentive owners will have to cooperate and help the production company with unexpected problems. As with everything else in life, production companies get what they pay for.

Other hidden location costs include the repair or replacement of expensive furnishings, decor, and landscaping that have been damaged by the crew. If a location is free but an overly picky owner demands that his or her lawn be replanted due to a few small tire marks, the location will become very expensive indeed. Money should be budgeted to repair damages or to soothe the frazzled nerves of an owner after the shoot has been completed, when the unavoidable nicks, dings, scratches, and smudges are discovered.

An owner's utility bills must also be regarded as part of the location expense. The crew runs in and out of a house a lot during a production. Electric cables must be run through outside doorways and windows, requiring that they be left open and forcing the heat or air-conditioning to operate all day. The consequences might not be so terrible for a short shoot, but if a location is occupied for several days or even weeks during a period of severe weather, fuel bills will climb surprisingly high. The owner may not discover this cost until long after the production company has left, and receiving a gas bill triple the regular amount can be a hair-raising surprise. A good location manager will bring up the subject on the shoot day and offer an extra fee to cover the increased utility use. It may be best for the location manager not to mention this prior to the shoot day, however, because it can provoke fears of giant unpaid utility bills and possibly scare the owner away.

The same is true for the telephone. Although the vast majority of crews will respect the owner's telephone and not charge long-distance calls to his or her account, there is the possibility that, even unintentionally, the production crew could run up hundreds of dollars in charges to an owner's account. The location manager would be well advised to soothe an owner's fears—again, preferably on the shooting day—by asking permission to use the phone and promising to charge long-distance calls to credit cards.

The location manger should also offer to pay for any long-distance charges that accidentally end up on the owner's bill and show good faith by adding another $50 to the fee if much phone use is expected. It will buy some goodwill and trust from the owner on the shooting day, when it will be needed most. Finally, it is extremely rare for owners to follow up on any long-distance calls that subsequently appear on their bill. If they have been paid a fair fee and otherwise treated well, they will overlook a small increase in any utility or phone bill.

If the location uses a well or septic tank, the increased load on those two systems could cause some trouble or delayed expense. Because the location manager does not want a plumbing failure on the shoot day, it would never hurt for him or her to ask about the condition or capacity of the systems and make arrangements for additional water and portable toilets if there is any concern.

In some cases, opportunistic neighbors can make such a fuss about the activity and disruption that they will need to be paid something to secure their cooperation. On any but the smallest productions, it is almost inevitable that someone will appear with the bright idea of taking advantage of the production company. Paying such individuals off quietly is generally the most expedient solution. But if news spreads that the production company is handing out money, the resulting envy and inevitable stampede will quickly wreck both the budget and the shoot. In any location situation where there are lots of neighbors, it is always wise to budget several hundred dollars for "uncooperative attitude adjustment expenses"—otherwise known as bribes.

THE LOCATION CONTRACT

A location contract can consist of anything from a handshake and a $50 bill to a hundred-page document signed off on by as many lawyers. Most common is the single-page *location release* (see Figure 6.2), which, at its simplest, includes the following information:

1. Name and address of the location
2. Subject of the shoot or title of the program in which the location will appear
3. Name and address of the production company
4. Dates of the shoot
5. A statement by the production company accepting liability for its activities while on location
6. A statement by the location owner giving permission to have photos or motion pictures of his or her property exhibited to the public in connection with the specified program

This information should not require pages of claims and disclaimers, but many lawyers, especially for large production companies, will insist on carte blanche in their location contracts or releases. They will attempt to duck any responsibility and liability while demanding the right to everything. As a result, many location releases can sound as if the location owner were signing away all imaginable rights. This approach can rub many property owners the wrong way.

Among the most serious objects of contention in a location release is the production company's frequent stipulation that it owns all rights to the photography and may use it in any way it wants, anywhere, forever. Location owners can find this clause frightening because they interpret it to mean that the footage of their home could one day appear in a program they regard as

LOCATION RELEASE

Date: _____

Location name: _____

Program title: _____

Production company: _____

Occupancy dates: _____

• •

I hereby agree that persons designated by the production company may occupy and use the above-named premises ("Location") on the above dates for the purpose of preparing for or making motion pictures, sound recordings, and/or photographs of the location in connection with the above-named program.

The production company accepts all responsibility for any property damage occurring to the location or for injury to any person on the premises that might occur as a direct result of the production company's occupancy of the location. The production company shall leave the location in at least the same condition as it was prior to its occupancy, except for usual and reasonable wear and tear.

I understand that the production company may edit recordings as it wishes and may include them or not include them in the program at its sole discretion. I understand that the program may be shown to the general public including over broadcast television networks, in movie theaters, and on home video.

The production company and/or anyone else it chooses will own all rights to, interest in, and copyright to the recordings made on the location. The production company may exhibit the recordings to the general public, without any limitation.

I represent that I have the legal right to make this agreement, and that the rights I grant will not infringe upon any rights of any other person or entity, or violate any existing commitment or agreement that would govern the use of the location.

_____

Print name and mailing address

_____   _____

For location   Date

_____   _____

For production company   Date

Figure 6.2 Sample location release.

offensive. Many people and businesses will balk at such an inclusive clause.

The production company only wants to be sure that owners understand that the footage of their property might appear on a poster or in some other publicity material such as a TV spot or trailer advertising the program. But when this simple requirement is translated into legalese by an overzealous lawyer, the wording becomes much more unpleasant. Many releases go on for paragraphs affirming the producer's sole rights "in all media currently in use or contemplated or ever to be invented throughout the known universe and possible universes yet to be discovered." Talk about tying it up. Suppose someone discovers a new dimension—then what?

This sort of complicated boilerplate will likely scare off the friendly corner grocer who has the perfect location. The solution is for the location manager to go to the producer or production manager and explain that the location release must be modified. With a bit of persistence, the release will be modified, especially if the director wants the location desperately enough. As society becomes more lawsuit-conscious, releases are making increasingly greater demands on location owners. One release used by a major Hollywood studio requires that location owners waive all rights to sue the studio *even* in the event of a breach of contract by the studio. That's nerve.

The solution is for location people to create a friendly release of their own. If the production company demands the use of its form, then at the slightest sign of the property owner's balking, the release should go back to the production office for revision. Most people are fearful of signing any contract, particularly one full of legalese. A one-sided location release will lose a good potential location quicker than almost anything else. Also, location people should resist accusations by the production company that they are incompetent because they could not get a property owner to sign an outrageous location release. Certain producers and production managers frequently need a good dose of the real world in which location people must spend most of their time.

THE COSTS AND BENEFITS OF ALTERING A LOCATION

The "perfect" location is never really perfect. It will always need something done to make it work in the scene. This could range from a simple straightening up to a major face-lift involving new rugs, wallpaper, and furnishings or even the removal of walls, doors, and windows.

At the very least, most of a home's furniture must be moved to make room for all the lighting, camera, and sound equipment. Doorways are often just an inch too narrow to accommodate larger pieces of film equipment, and so the doors must be taken off of their hinges. A chandelier or any type of hanging light fixture is a problem because it casts unwanted shadows and often obstructs the movement of the sound boom. Windows that appear in a shot may need sheer curtains to soften the light or mask an unwanted view.

Sofas, chairs, pianos, china cabinets—all might need to be removed to create a less cluttered look for the camera. If a picture with a glass front is kicking light back at a bad angle, another picture might have to be substituted. A mirror might be in the shot, reflecting the images of the camera and crew. It, too, must go. This sort of rearranging will make any owner nervous.

If the script calls for pieces of furniture other than or in addition to the location's existing furnishings, they will need to be brought in. Some locations will retain only a small portion of their original look, which is very surprising to the owners. They will certainly wonder why their house was picked in the first place if it required such a transformation.

These are some of the simplest situations. When the production involves a period setting, even more drastic changes can be required. The lobby of a turn-of-the-century office building might be decorated to look like the waiting room of a train station. The dining room of a Victorian mansion might be decorated to look like an office in the White House. A period film might call for a complete change of wallpaper, window treatments, trim paint, and rugs—sometimes followed by a complete change back again. Although that can be expensive, it is still not as expensive as renting a studio and building a set from scratch. This is especially true with feature films shot on distant locations where no studio space is available.

With exterior locations, the weather might not be right. A blizzard might need to be staged in the middle of July, requiring that someone's lawn be heaped with fake snow and cotton/Styrofoam drifts. Homes might have to be aged and distressed, or they might have to be spruced up. Plants might be added and bushes ripped up. Trees might require trimming or even complete removal. A brown lawn might need to be dyed green (yes, it happens all the time without harm).

It can actually be best to have the location owners present throughout the whole process of moving furniture and other decorations. If the owners watch as their lovely living room is dismantled bit by bit and the furnishings carefully placed out of harm's way, they can adjust slowly. If they come in to see their entire house totally rearranged and loaded with rough-looking production equipment, the shock can be overwhelming.

In any case, location managers must warn property owners in advance about even these minor changes. But they need to do it gently and without alarm. They should avoid making a big issue out of it and stress that everyone involved is an experienced professional. Describing in detail the changes a house will undergo to accommodate a crew will discourage most owners. Besides, good crews are remarkably adept at putting a location back the way they found it. Location people must always promise to return the location to *a condition as good as, if not better than, its original condition*—and be sure that this is done.

Permanent Alterations to a Location

Sometimes, it is necessary to permanently alter the interior or exterior of a location. Outside, this can include removing a tree limb or an entire tree. It can involve repainting; cutting a mail slot; updating a door; adding a fountain, balcony, or porch.

Inside, it can include renovating a kitchen or bathroom, painting and papering, adding light fixtures, or finishing a basement.

These types of permanent alterations are expensive enough to begin with, but they become much more expensive if the location will need to be returned to its original state after filming—which can be impossible, particularly in the case of tree and shrub removal. Therefore, the goal is to convince the location owner that the permanent alteration is a valuable *improvement* to the property and should be left after the shooting has finished. Sometimes, this approach works, and the alterations can be considered as part of the location fee or even as full payment of the fee.

Problems arise when location owners do not particularly want or even like the alterations. They may not like the color of the paint or wall paper. They may not like the new design of the kitchen. They may not want their wooden screen door replaced with a garish aluminum one. They may prefer the way their tree looks with all its branches, even though it might be in desperate need of trimming.

If the production company is lucky and the script requirements match the location owners' tastes, then everyone benefits. If the owners will not budge on essential changes, then the location people must consider looking for a more suitable site. They should approach the owners as early as possible about permanent alterations, so that alternate sites can be found in case there is disagreement. It is a bad idea for location people to show up and suddenly announce to the owners that their rose garden must be replaced by a child's swing set.

RELATIONS WITH NEIGHBORS

Good relations with nearby neighbors are the linchpin on which all location shoots turn. Neighbors can be a wild card and are the cause of the most serious location problems. The location manager must pay close attention to those who might be affected by the production activity and either see that their needs are met in some way or see that they do not slow the production down, stop it, or have any other adverse effect on it.

Shooting long-form dramas, such as feature films and television movies, and TV commercials involves intense activities. The people, equipment, vehicles, and actual shooting can be quite disruptive to neighbors in a number of ways:

- Production vehicles can occupy the parking places normally used by people in a neighborhood, forcing them to walk a distance from their cars to their homes.
- If the production is shooting on a street, traffic may have to be rerouted, making it inconvenient or impossible for visitors or delivery persons to approach houses near the location. Rerouted traffic also means backups and traffic jams, which anger many people.
- If the shoot requires sound recording, people in the neighborhood must suspend noisy activities, which include using any kind of power equipment such as lawn mowers, chain saws, drills, sanders, cement mixers, or tillers; loud play by children; barking dogs; home repairs or construction; car maintenance—in fact, just about anything anyone does outside except sleep in a hammock.
- To avoid ruining a shot, bystanders cannot be allowed to chat or to stand where they might accidentally appear in the scene, and neighbors may not be allowed to come out of their houses.
- Neighbors may, on short notice, be asked to move their cars or their lawn furniture, or to turn their lights on or off, because those things appear in the shot and are inappropriate for some reason.
- The general activity of the production crew on a night shoot can be very disturbing to residents who are trying to sleep. The bright lights, generator noise, walkie-talkie chatter, crew talk, and noisy special effects—explosions, the screeching of car tires, fireworks, or gunshots—can keep neighbors awake all night.

- The presence of a production can draw many curious onlookers from outside a neighborhood who add to the noise and confusion. These types can be unruly and may even damage neighbors' property in their attempts to get a glimpse of the action.
- Businesses will strongly object if customers cannot easily enter their premises because access is blocked by production crews and their equipment or shots.

All the above are major considerations that will occupy the majority of the location team's energies. Their negative effects can be minimized by proper communication with the neighbors, common courtesy, and quick thinking.

The Large Exterior Shoot

The most difficult situation is the large exterior shoot. All the problems discussed in the preceding subsection will come into play, and the location manager must be prepared to deal with them. The first step, always, is to enlist the help of the local film commission or other public authorities (police, traffic department, mayor's office). The shot and the needs of the production are explained to them, and if they feel that complying with the request will not produce too much disruption, then they will cooperate.

After receiving official permission, the location manager must next contact the business owners and residents who will be most directly affected by the production. This is generally done by placing a *location letter* (see Figure 6.3) on the front door of each affected premise. This letter informs the owner of the following details:

- The dates and times of the shoot
- Whether owners will be asked to do or not do certain things such as move their cars or refrain from cutting their grass (noise factor)

Zebra Productions, Inc.

11677 Overland Mall Rd., Charlotte, NC 88888 / 704-555-1674

March 14, 1994

Dear Walnut Street Resident,

Zebra Productions, Inc., is considering filming a TV commercial in the 400 block of Walnut Street next week. The commercial is for Golden Dairies and will be broadcast over local television stations.

We picked your block because all of the houses have an authentic 1940s look, and the commercial takes place in that time period. The scene shows a milkman on his morning rounds, delivering Golden Dairies milk from his 1942 truck.

The main action will take place in front of the Wilgus residence at 411 Walnut Street. They requested that we contact all the neighbors who might be affected by the filming to be sure that no one had problems with it. We will arrive at 7:00 A.M. on Wednesday, March 23, and finish by about 5:00 P.M. Approximately 30 people will be working on the commercial. There will be several large trucks that carry all the lights, cameras, props, and the like. These trucks will be parked opposite the Wilgus home.

Because we will need to drive the milk delivery truck down the street, the street will be closed to through traffic most of the day. The Police Department has granted tentative permission for this. There are many breaks in filming, so local residents and deliveries will be able to get through with no problem. Production assistants stationed at the ends of the block will alert drivers to the situation.

Filming a commercial can be very interesting, and you are welcome to watch. A production assistant will let you know if you are in "camera range."

Finally, because we're trying to create a 1940s-period look, we ask that you not park cars on the street that day. Please use your garage. If that is any problem please let me know, and I can make special arrangements.

If you have any concerns about the filming, or have questions, please call me any time, day or night, at **555-1674**, and I will be happy to help. If I do not hear from you by March 16, I will assume that everything is fine. We will contact you the day before the filming to confirm that we will be coming.

Thank you in advance for your patience and cooperation, and we hope you will enjoy your "day in Hollywood."

Sincerely yours,

Robert Maier
Location Manager

Figure 6.3 Sample location letter.

- The extent and nature of the disruption (e.g., street or sidewalk closure, helicopter hovering, stunt, gunshots)
- Arrangements made by the production company to meet the residents' needs (e.g., special parking, special trash collection, escort to school buses)
- The name of the production company and the name and number of someone whom residents can contact if they have any questions, problems, or special needs

This letter, possibly with an endorsement by the local authorities, should be delivered several days or a week before the shoot, and earlier if possible. People will need time to consider how a street closure may affect such activities as furniture deliveries, home repairs, or plans to be away from home. If the activities and cooperation of neighbors are particularly critical—for example, their homes or businesses will appear in a shot—then the letter must be followed up with an in-person visit by someone from the location staff. Letters get lost, forgotten, or ignored, and the location manager must be absolutely certain that he or she will have the full cooperation of every person whose property will appear in the shot.

If there are any schedule changes, all the affected residents must be notified as soon as possible. They must also be reminded of the pending shoot shortly before it is to take place, definitely the night before. If a schedule changes frequently and there are many neighbors to inform, this becomes a large undertaking and requires additional production assistants to accomplish. A good motto is to "Tell them once, tell them again, and then tell them one more time." It is amazing how quickly people forget.

A personal visit also allows the location staff to get the *name, street address, and phone number of all the affected individuals* so they can be called quickly at a later date with information updates or schedule changes. A little map noting the name and phone number of each person will come in handy during the shoot and will impress the ADs who might need to ask that a slight change be made to a house before the camera rolls.

Finally, it is wise to obtain a location release in advance from owners of all the affected homes, even if their property only appears in the background. On the shooting day, things will simply be too hectic for paperwork. Also, there could be some ruffled feathers on that day, and people might be a little less cooperative about signing a release.

Businesses as Neighbors

Warning! Businesses require special attention. Small entre-preneurs—grocers, dry cleaners, gas station owners, and so forth—can easily be overlooked and take great offense when their business is affected by a production. They will complain bitterly to anyone who will listen—police, elected officials, or news media—that they are being put out of business by a production. Many have short tempers, a taste for cash, and brothers-in-law who are lawyers. Owners of affected busi-nesses should be paid a reasonable amount in consideration of their potential losses, and the production company should obtain from them, up front, a written agreement stating their consent to avoid a misunderstanding later on.

Local Services

Location managers must be aware of mail delivery times, trash pickup, school bus service, UPS and other delivery services, and home maintenance/repair people when scheduling and planning the shoot. They must be familiar with the needs of every single affected property owner. This is usually easy, because most people come and go in the normal 9:00 to 5:00 routine, and the production can work uninterrupted in most residential districts, except during morning and evening rush hours.

The safest way to avoid problems with local services is for someone from the location department to speak with every affected property owner individually. Not only will the owners' needs be discovered, but they will doubtless be won over by the location department's show of concern.

Noise and Other Interruptions to the Neighborhood

It is the responsibility of the location department to intervene when neighbors begin some sort of activity that disrupts a production. This includes any noisy activity (such as mowing the lawn, hammering nails, or revving a car engine) as well as gawking at the camera from the background of a shot. Directors swear that pilots of small planes purposely buzz their set to gawk and will demand that the location manager call the airport and have the pilots ordered away.

In the case of noisy or otherwise intrusive neighbors, a pleasant manner and polite request will go a long way. Most people are sympathetic and may even be embarrassed about having interrupted the production's work. On the other hand, there are some people who have a busy schedule or are just hostile and uncooperative.

If the noise makers are paid workers such as construction crews, it is difficult to make them stop their work completely. After all, no supervisor wants to have his or her workers standing around idly while the time clock is ticking. But compromises can be arranged. Work crews might be able to schedule their noisy activities—sawing, drilling, hammering—between sound takes. This requires posting a production assistant with a walkie-talkie next to the workers. The PA will cue them to start and stop according to the directions of the ADs. An hour of production time might require only a few minutes of sound recording, so the "noisy" workers will not be excessively delayed. Also, a little present of cold soda and some snacks from the crafts service table will buy lots of gracious cooperation from most workers.

In cases where polite requests and small favors will not sway an intruder, then money might be the only solution. A $50 bill slipped to an ornery neighbor can save the production thousands of dollars in overtime. A good location manager will have an array of little inducements and thank-yous at hand, consisting of bouquets of flowers, cases of beer and soda, restaurant gift certificates, autographed photos of stars, crew T-shirts, and a wallet full of tens and twenties.

If a neighbor is completely uncooperative and belligerent, then the next step is to request help from the police, who will usually convince even the biggest jerk that it is in his or her best interest to leave the production alone. Very rarely, even the police can be powerless. If that is the case, then the production's only recourse is to try to buy the offender off with big money, live with the distraction, or shift the location. However, such situations are pretty rare.

If a serious problem arises, then the location manager can be blamed for not having identified the problem early and solved it before the shooting crew arrived. Sometimes, even the best scouting and preparation will fail to detect the presence of an uncooperative neighbor until too late. Then, the location manager can only hope for understanding from the production staff. "Civilians" are not as predictable or controllable as a professional crew. One of the primary drawbacks of location management is the possibility of intrusion by an uncooperative outside world—and the impatience of producers, directors, and assistant directors when such external interruptions do occur.

7

Location Support

LOCAL VENDORS

A production company that is on location often seems like a self-contained village. It has a mobile kitchen, dressing rooms, medic, electric power plants, air-conditioned office trailers, and equipment trucks with hundreds of lights and miles of cable. It has fuel trucks; prop trucks; and machine, carpentry, and welding shops. It has fully equipped hair salons, bathrooms, a sewing shop, and even a laundry. The crafts service table is like a little hotel kiosk offering a wide variety of snacks, drinks, vitamins, medicines, other personal products, and maybe even the daily papers. But the production company cannot provide everything. It needs outside support.

The local location support vendors are suppliers that a production will need when its own supplies and equipment are insufficient for a particular situation. Even in the largest production, there will be times when someone requires some oddball thing and will turn to the location department to find it. It is the location department's responsibility to provide a list of suppliers that are closest to the location. A *location support form* (see Figure 7.1) is used to keep track of these suppliers.

Only larger productions need very detailed information, but even on a small TV spot, it is an excellent idea for someone from the location department to drive around an unfamiliar neighborhood to discover what kinds of stores or services are nearby, just in case. The most common location support needs are:

- *Convenience store*: Such stores carry a surprising variety of goods, including drinks, medicine, extension cords, and shoe polish. Many have fax machines, photocopiers, gas pumps, and money machines. They are quick and easy. A well-stocked convenience store can handle 90 percent of a location's local support needs.
- *Hardware store/lumberyard*: The grip/electric and art departments will always need some exotic fitting, paint, or piece of wood, which can be obtained from a hardware store or lumberyard.
- *Grocery store*: Basically, grocery stores are an expanded version of convenience stores, but they can be too slow or far away for fast runs, or their hours can be too limited. They do offer a much wider selection and better prices though.
- *Shopping center*: Closest mall, discount warehouse, or other department store.
- *Hospital*: This is very important in case of an emergency. Someone in the location department should have driven the route to the hospital in advance and must be available to drive there if needed.
- *Photocopier/printer*: Daily call sheets are often typed and need to be distributed on location at the last minute. The best bet will be a small print shop, if one is nearby—preferably, a shop with equipment that can print or copy on both sides of the page and do size reductions. A deal can sometimes be made with a small local business to use its equipment if no commercial copy shop is available, but access must be fast

LOCATION SUPPORT

Location: _____

_____

_____

Scene: _____

Date: _____

	Address	Hours	Phone	Miles/ Minutes
Convenience store:	_____	_____	_____	_____
	_____			
Hardware store:	_____	_____	_____	_____
	_____			
Grocery store:	_____	_____	_____	_____
	_____			
Shopping center:	_____	_____	_____	_____
	_____			
Hospital:	_____	_____	_____	_____
	_____			
Photocopier:	_____	_____	_____	_____
	_____			
Fax:	_____	_____	_____	_____
	_____			
Pay phone:	_____	_____	_____	_____
	_____			
_____:	_____	_____	_____	_____
	_____			

SECOND-MEAL PLACES
(See back for map/directions.)

Figure 7.1 Sample location support form.

and easy. The ADs will need to make copies of call sheets at every location, so the location department must be prepared.

- *Fax*: Closest business where emergency faxes can be sent and received.
- *Second-meal places*: The caterer has usually departed by the time wrap comes, but five to six hours might have passed since lunch—and crafts service snacks won't do. A "second meal" will be called for, and it needs to be something hot. Sandwich shops, fried chicken and Chinese carryouts, and pizza joints are familiar late-night haunts of productions that run into unexpected overtime. In more sophisticated areas, even Thai, Japanese, or Middle Eastern carryouts may be available. The assistant directors will expect the location department to have menus from a number of fast, nearby carryout places.
- *Pay phone*: Although pay phones are becoming less important in the age of cellular phones, knowing the location of the closest pay phone is critical. Someone from the location department should be sure to test that the pay phone works for both incoming and outgoing calls, and the production office should be given the number.

Some less important but helpful places for the location department to keep an eye out for include a laundromat, a one-hour photo developer, a liquor store (for VIP entertainment and the crew's wrap beer), and fire and police stations. In a completely strange location with a small crew, it is good to know the nearest production equipment rental house and production company for help, advice, and understanding from kindred souls. These companies usually will be listed in the local yellow pages.

If a production will be filming in a particular area for a while, it is important for the location manager to carry a copy of the local yellow pages. People will need to find everything from heavy-equipment rental companies to septic tank cleaners, and they will come to the location manager for that information.

BASE-CAMP REQUIREMENTS

As noted before, a location shoot creates its own minivillage. The central "village square" where all the support vehicles— the trailers, equipment trucks, honey wagons, caterer, and crafts service—are located is called the *base camp*. The actual shooting set may be several hundred yards or more away because it is on a site that is inaccessible to the larger production vehicles. In these situations, people and gear are shuttled to and from the set in cars, pickup trucks, and electric golf carts.

The location manager has several concerns when setting up the base camp. Because the base camp consists almost exclusively of production vehicles, it is primarily the responsibility of the transportation department. However, the transportation department will rely on the location department to supply many needs, and there must be close and regular communication between both departments to avoid not just traffic jams but a situation in which an awkwardly organized base camp slows down a production and wastes money.

Production Vehicle Parking

Parking is the primary consideration in setting up a base camp. Literally hundreds of feet of curb space are required to accommodate a fleet that, on the average feature film, will include:

- Lighting/electric production van (65 feet)
- Grip truck (40 feet)
- Honey wagon (mobile dressing-room tractor-trailer, 65 feet)
- Star trailers/mobile homes (35 feet)
- Wardrobe trailer (35 feet)
- Hair/makeup trailer (35 feet)

- Prop truck (14 feet)
- Set dress truck (25 feet)
- Sound cargo van
- Camera truck (21 feet)
- Crafts service van
- Cast passenger van
- Two or three pickup trucks

The base camp has to accommodate all these vehicles in an orderly manner. Of course, these are only the base-camp vehicles. Personal cars (discussed later in the chapter) also must be considered.

Electricity

A base camp will require a significant amount of electric power to run all the production machinery, including power tools, washers/dryers, work and practical lighting, and rather hefty heat and air-conditioning units for all the dressing rooms. Each vehicle or trailer may have its own electric power generator, but the combination of five or six mildly muffled diesel motors creates a nerve-racking rumble that might even disturb a distant shooting set. Usually, though, the honey wagon will have a large enough generator and plenty of cable to power an entire base camp, and it will have sufficient noise damping to keep the ambient sound to a tolerable level.

Other drawbacks to generators are that they are rather delicate machines that tend to break down and require servicing several times a week. Generators also burn a substantial amount of fuel when they run twelve to fourteen hours a day six days a week. Fuel costs can reach several hundred dollars per week, and the regular refueling of half a dozen units can be a nuisance. Generators have a habit of running out of fuel or breaking down at the most unfortunate times, and a dollar's worth of bad fuel or a clogged fuel line can stop a production dead in its tracks.

The simplest solution for obtaining electricity is to arrange for a *temporary power drop* from the closest utility pole. A temporary drop is a power line strung to a pole with a meter and circuit-breaker box attached. It will provide all the power a base camp will need—quietly, reliably, and cheaply. However, a drop is only cost-effective if a base camp will be used for several days because it costs several hundred dollars to install it. Local power companies will assist with a temporary drop and will be happy to help arrange it with only a few days' notice.

A temporary drop is not a perfect solution, particularly in rural areas where power is regularly knocked out for hours in bad weather. In these situations, it is wise to have sufficient generator power as a backup.

Motor Fuels

All the base camp's electric generators are prodigious guzzlers of diesel fuel and regular gasoline and must be refilled regularly. The vehicles themselves will also need fuel, although not as frequently as the generators. This service is performed by a fuel oil company that will deliver on-site with a medium-size tanker truck. For large productions, a running account will be arranged by the transportation manager. The location manager's primary consideration in this area is to realize that the fuel tanker must have easy access to the vehicles requiring fuel.

Some productions will rent a pickup truck known as a "fueler," which has in its rear bed a pump and a custom fuel tank with a capacity of 500 or more gallons. This nifty vehicle can easily navigate the maze of trucks, tractors, and trailers and assures a constant emergency backup supply of fuel.

Water

Honey wagons, makeup trailers, wardrobe trailers—all need significant amounts of water, primarily for flush toilets and sinks. They have large holding tanks, which must be refilled on location at least several times a week. A fire hydrant is the best source of water (provided there is one nearby), and transportation departments have the tools to open fire hydrants and draw water from them. However, some local governments require a permit and may charge a fee for hydrant use, so it is important for the location department to check with the local water department before using hydrants.

The second best source of water is the outside spigot of a residence or business. Even though a base camp could draw hundreds of gallons of water for its various tanks, it will not greatly increase the owner's water bill. Paying someone $50 to use his or her hose for an hour or two is generous. The location department must be careful of homes that are on small wells, however. A honey wagon could easily overburden the wells and accidentally run them dry.

Finally, the location manager must always be aware of the distance between the water source and the honey wagon's planned parking area. Honey wagons are equipped with several hundred feet of hose, but in some cases, that may not be enough. It is a very big deal to move the honey wagon once it has been set up simply because its water hose is 25 feet too short.

Telephone

Larger productions live and die by the phone, and two or three lines on location would not be excessive for them. Even the smallest production needs at least one phone line close at hand all the time.

Most phone companies can run temporary telephone lines to a base camp with just several days' notice—especially if some strings are pulled. If a production is to be in a "phone-less" location for a week or more, it could save thousands of dollars by installing temporary phone lines. For shorter location occupations, the production company can offer to buy out an existing service—for example, pay for the use of the owner's or a friendly neighbor's phone.

Nearby pay phones, if not too busy, are a good alternative, and the location manager should locate and check out any that are within a five-minute walk. Of course, cellular phones are the easiest solution (particularly in urban areas), but they are much more expensive than landlines and are a viable option only if the production company can afford the tab.

Sewage

Yes, unpleasant as it is, base camps, like any little village, even generate sewage. Because the water from the clothes-washer outlet in the wardrobe trailer is not toxic, it might be directed into the nearest storm drain (although rigs designed in a more environmentally conscious manner will have a holding tank). The legality of putting *any* water down a storm drain should be checked first, however.

Because of their extensive toilet and washbowl facilities, the honey wagon, motor home, and star trailers will have septic holding tanks that must be emptied regularly into an approved dump station. A more convenient method is to have a septic cleaning tank truck come to the base camp to drain the holding tanks. As is the case with refueling, the location manager must be sure that there is easy access to the honey wagons for this purpose, although this responsibility is shared with the transportation department.

EXTRAS HOLDING AREAS

Holding areas are normally considered a part of the base camp but are under the control of the location department, not the transportation department. A *holding area* is simply a room (or rooms) where extras wait for their set call. In any size production, be it a TV spot or a Hollywood extravaganza, if extras are used, then they must have a holding area.

Extras spend most of their time waiting to go on set, which amounts to many hours in the workday. They must always be on standby to be brought to the set on a moment's notice. Some days they may not even be brought to the set at all! But because they are always on call, they cannot be allowed to wander off where they might miss the call, damage their costume, or spoil their makeup. This may sound silly, but dealing with a large, bored crowd, which can often be made up of nonprofessionals, is no simple job. If the extras are union members, there are strict rules about how they are to be treated. The production company can actually be fined by the Screen Actors Guild if the extras are not provided with the union-stipulated facilities.

The extras holding area must be clean and comfortable, with chairs and tables. It must be air-conditioned or heated, depending on the weather. It must be sheltered from any rain, snow, and so forth. Because extras may need to change into costumes, private men's and women's dressing rooms must be provided. Extras cannot take their personal clothing and belongings, including wallets and purses, to the set, so there must be a secure, guarded area for these valuables. Tables and chairs must be provided for a sit-down lunch as well as for general chatting, card games, crossword puzzles, telephoning, resting, script writing—all of the activities that help extras while away their waiting time.

The best extras holding areas are large rooms like church basements, volunteer fire halls, Elks Clubs, and other types of meeting rooms. Such facilities have rest rooms and plenty of tables and chairs. They are also clean, easily accessible, and may even have pay phones. It is best to have the holding area a short walk from the set—far enough away that noise will not be a factor. If the holding area is too distant, though, a shuttle bus might be required. Second ADs will guide the extras to the set when needed, obtaining their instructions from the set via walkie-talkies.

Crafts service will set up an extras table in the holding area to provide snacks and drinks. It will often serve as the crew's eating area during meal breaks. The hair, makeup, and wardrobe departments will sometimes set up satellite operations in the holding area exclusively to handle extras.

The extras holding area is therefore an active place. Between the crew meals, the application of makeup, and the presence of lounging extras, it can become quite a mess at the end of the day and will require some serious cleanup attention—which is the responsibility of the location staff.

One final note: The holding area has to be treated as a location. Its owner must be given a call time, and access must be assured when the extras show up in the morning so that they can be gotten into wardrobe and makeup without delay. Getting fifty or more extras ready can take several hours, and the location department does not want to be blamed for delaying the shoot because the holding area is locked. It is often best for the location manager to obtain a key to the holding area because the first extras' call on a big movie often is scheduled for some unholy hour like 4:00 A.M.—earlier than most "civilians" want to arrive anywhere.

CAST AND CREW PARKING

Although the tangle of the base camp and the demands of the extras holding area are daunting enough by themselves, crew parking must then be added to the situation. Most people take parking for granted, and it would seem on the surface not to be a serious issue—but in fact, it can be a big problem. Over the course of a large film, many hours can be lost, at a cost of many thousands of dollars, if parking is not adequately planned.

Almost everyone drives his or her own vehicle to work, so besides all the production trucks and vans, a location manager must also be prepared to provide parking for several dozen cast and crew cars; and if many extras are involved, maybe another hundred. In some difficult situations, shuttle buses, under the supervision of the transportation department, might be needed to get everyone from the parking lot to the base camp.

Parking must be nearby and easy to find. If people have a hard time finding the parking area, the day's start will be delayed, with only the lax location manager to blame. Crew members may need to carry tools or other heavy items to the set and do not want to park a mile away, so the closer the parking area, the better. In certain areas where there is no off-street parking, the local authorities will often grant special curb or on-street parking permits to production crews for a short term. In residential neighborhoods, occupying the local people's parking spots will definitely ruffle feathers, and people whose normal spots are taken over by a production must be considered and provided for as well.

Parking must be organized. When the production calls for dozens or hundreds of extras, parking is most important. And if only a small lot is available, the parking area might not have the convenience of a mall. In such cases, the cars need to be packed in as tightly as possible, as in a big-city parking lot. This requires the services of a parking expert—someone who can jockey cars around without banging them up. Having an expert is particularly worthwhile if extras are dismissed in a trickle and one "buried" car after another must be extracted from the lot. Any delays will cost the production in hefty overtime payments.

Parking, whether in a lot or on the street, must be secure. In bad neighborhoods, a fleet of strange, unprotected cars is an irresistible lure to petty thieves and vandals. Nothing will sour overworked crew members at the end of a fourteen-hour day more than discovering that the battery or radio has been stolen from their car or its tires have been slashed.

In fact, many experienced crew members who have had security problems before will make a very big issue of parking near the set or base camp and cause a nasty scene if they are not granted a close spot. The location manager must therefore provide either a production assistant or a professional security guard to patrol the cars at all times. This is why it is best for the production company to either buy out some sort of lot or get permission to use a long, unbroken stretch of on-street parking. If all the production cars are kept together, it is much easier and cheaper to keep them secure. On many productions, the closest parking spots must be reserved for the VIPs (producers, director, stars).

Two final notes about parking: First, where there are many cars, it is inevitable that some people will lose their keys or lock them inside their car. Where cars have been tightly packed, a keyless car or a car that refuses to start can be a major obstacle to clearing the lot—again, causing expensive delays. Good transportation departments can help here with battery jumper cables and not-quite-legal hot-wire equipment or "slim jim" car door openers. These simple tools and the skill to use them correctly can save hundreds of labor hours, not to mention frayed tempers. The location manager should at least have a set of jumper cables and a few metal coat hangers stashed in his or her trunk for the inevitable dead battery or car lockout situations.

Second, parking areas must be treated as an important enough element to appear on a call sheet, and the parking lot owner must be continually updated about the shooting schedule. Many lots have a locking gate, which will need to be open for the earliest call. Having a parking lot that no one can get into because the gate is chained and locked is a disaster that can set an entire shooting day behind. In fact, an important tool for a location manager is a good chain cutter or hacksaw for those occasions when someone forgets to unlock a chained gate. Ruining a $20 lock is much less expensive than incurring an hour of overtime that might cost $5,000.

MAPS AND DIRECTIONS TO THE LOCATION

Before people can actually get to a location, they need to know where it is. And because the location department found the location in the first place, it makes sense for its staff to tell everyone else how to get there. We all know how difficult it is to give directions to someone completely unfamiliar with an area. Crews are easily confused by strange areas, and because they are on the clock, proper directions provided by the location department are critical to having the workday begin smoothly.

The first step in providing directions is for someone from the location department to obtain the most detailed map of an area. Nearly every county and city has a published map that shows detail down to the smallest alley or even footpath. These maps, which can be purchased at local convenience stores, are usually excellent. As good as they are, however, such maps cannot be relied on completely because cartographers do make mistakes—for example, connecting roads that never actually join, misnaming roads, or leaving out existing roads. Mistakes like these are rare, but they do occur, and the location manager cannot blame an incorrect map when a shoot is delayed by a lost crew.

The solution is for the location manager to actually drive the route, using the map as a guide. By doing so, he or she will be able to spot any errors the map may contain. Furthermore, even if a map is perfect, there might be other problems that can only be discovered by driving the route—roads under construction or one-way streets that are not marked as such on the map. If new bypasses or intersections have been built since the map was published, the map might be entirely wrong or an easier, faster route might now exist.

Trucks will need their own sets of directions. Particularly in urban areas, there are many strictly designated truck and nontruck routes such as parkways, shopping districts, and quiet residential areas. Production trucks might also exceed weight restrictions on older bridges and roads and be forced to take a detour using an entirely different route.

The location manager must drive the route from the departure point of the crew. This could be from the hotel where crew members are staying or from a studio where other parts of the shoot are based; it may need to be from both. Sometimes, large crews are based at two or three widely separated hotels, and because the route to the location from each hotel would be entirely different, directions from each are needed.

To make things even more difficult, the return route from location to home base is often different. This can be due to the presence of one-way streets or different entrances and exits on high-speed roadways; but there are other tricky situations that can result in a different return route, so the entire route must be retraced. Also, on a shoot day that will involve a location change, most people will need to know how to get from one location to another most efficiently. The location department must provide directions and maps for those trips as well.

Making Directions

So, many sets of directions are needed. It is time consuming to provide all the different versions, so creating them should be accomplished as efficiently as possible. This requires some foresight and a few tools. At this point, location managers should already know how to get to the location, and now they are simply documenting the details so that others will be able to find it as quickly as possible.

The tools they need are the aforementioned detailed map of the area, a notepad, and a small cassette recorder. The most important of these is the cassette recorder. It is nearly impossible to take adequate written notes while driving on freeways or in any sort of traffic. It is much easier for location managers to dictate the directions into the recorder and then transcribe them later when sitting safely at a desk.

The best procedure is for location managers to begin at the first home base (hotel, studio). They zero the tripmeter on their car and take off. As they drive, they verbally note how far they have traveled, any pertinent landmarks, and the name of the streets where turns should be made. For example: "Drive west on Calvert Street. You will see an Exxon station on the left at .8 mile. This is Pratt Street. Make a right. Follow Pratt Street to the second flashing red light. There's a McDonald's on the corner. Make a left on to Howard Street."

It is a simple procedure—much easier than juggling a pen and paper. But location managers must be sure that their recorder is operating properly. I once spent a day driving around dictating directions only to find that the recorder had a malfunctioning switch and nothing had been recorded. The whole day was lost.

After returning to the office, location managers would be well advised to use a word processor to type the directions. On long shoots with many locations, certain portions of each direction sheet will be repeated either verbatim or perhaps with only minor changes. The word processor's ability to store and copy these repeated sections will save hours of typing. The directions should be laid out clearly and simply and include contact names and phone numbers, street addresses, and the name of the location in the script (see Figure 7.2).

Although written directions are sufficient, most drivers will also appreciate a basic map, which will usually fit on the same sheet as the directions. Location managers who want to be even more thorough can attach a copy of the applicable portion of the published road map for the area. This is a big help for those who might get lost but are still close to the location. They will usually be able to use that map to find where they are and see how to get back on track.

A day's directions package could include twenty or thirty pages and seven or eight slightly different versions of the directions. It can get confusing, so it is vital that each person receive the appropriate copy of the directions package. The location department must be sure it has plenty of copies of each, so it should allow enough time to photocopy, collate, and staple the map package. It is best not to give out the maps until the call sheets are distributed (too many people will lose them). The assistant directors usually will want to attach the directions packets to the call sheets anyway.

Finally, it is helpful to include a state or regional map with the first location directions package. Most film commissions have road maps that they will provide at no charge. They are never as detailed as the local topographic survey-

"CRYBABY" — DIRECTIONS TO LOCATION   Shoot date: _____

••

Location: **Cloisters Children's Museum** (Vernon-Williams Home)
              10440 Falls Rd. 21204 (Baltimore County)

••

In case of problem, call Location Dept. cellular phone – 555-1234
or "Crybaby" office at 555-1256
Location site cannot take messages or contact crew.

DIRECTIONS TO CLOISTERS FROM TREMONT PLAZA HOTEL:

• Take ST. PAUL ST. south to first stoplight, which is Lexington St.
  Make left turn.

• Follow LEXINGTON ST. to 4th stoplight, which is GAY ST. Make left turn.
  Quickly get into left curb lane.

• Follow GAY ST. approximately 50 yards, under expressway bridge.

• Make sharp left turn immediately past expressway bridge onto entrance
  ramp of I-83. (JONES FALLS EXPRESSWAY).

• Proceed on I-83 approximately 8 miles. At junction of I-695, continue on
  I-83 KEEP LEFT, FOLLOWING FALLS RD., RT. 25, and EXPRESSWAY
  ENDS signs. Come to a stoplight.

• At STOPLIGHT, make LEFT TURN onto FALLS RD.

• Follow FALLS RD. aproximately 6/10 mile—past HILLSIDE RD.

• Follow FALLS RD. 100 yards farther. ENTRANCE to Museum is on right.
  See **"Cloisters"** sign on left side of road, opposite entrance drive.

• Follow drive—keeping right at any turnoffs. Drive ends in parking area for
  crew vehicles.

••

RETURN FROM CLOISTERS TO TREMONT PLAZA HOTEL:

• At driveway entrance to FALLS RD., make left turn onto FALLS RD.

• Proceed on FALLS RD. approximately 5/10 mile.

• See road sign on right: "JONES FALLS EXPRESSWAY TO BALTIMORE
  BELTWAY AND I-83." Make right turn onto JONES FALLS EXPRESSWAY.

• Proceed on EXPRESSWAY approximately 8 miles to EXIT marked
  "ST. PAUL ST. – ROUTE 2.

• Proceed south on ST. PAUL ST. to CENTER ST. Bear right at fork onto
  ST. PAUL PLACE. Proceed on ST. PAUL PLACE approximately 5 blocks.
  TREMONT PLAZA HOTEL is on the right.

••

Notes:

SEE MAP ON BACK.

Figure 7.2 Sample directions to a location.

based maps, but they will give an overall view of the area and will come in handy more than once for the inevitable lost drivers.

INSURANCE

Production insurance is an insurance package purchased by the producer and the production manager to cover all the activities of a production. The portion of this package that is important to the location person is the policy that covers injury to persons and damage to others' property while the production is on location. It is known as the "liability policy" and basically says that the insurance company will pay for any loss incurred by anyone due to the activities of the production company. This includes everything from a production company's accidentally burning down a house to a grip's tripping over a location owner's bicycle and breaking an arm.

The policy covers only large-scale damage or injury because it usually has a deductible of several thousand dollars. Its coverage limit is commonly as high as $10 million, and the minimum is usually $1 million. In the event of minor injuries to people and small nicks and scratches to property, compensation is paid from the production funds, not the liability insurance. The purpose of the policy is to protect the location owner from serious financial loss should an expensive accident occur. As with all insurance, the deep-pocketed insurance company assumes all liability (for a hefty fee), and the location owner can rest assured that the bills will be paid.

All location owners will want this assurance before they will allow a production company on their property. The risks are too obvious and too great, particularly in this era of easy lawsuits and large settlements. Big cities require production companies to have at least $1 million in liability insurance before they will allow shooting on public property. In some instances—such as shoots at airports, in subways, or at other public places with heavy pedestrian traffic—$10 million will be required.

Insurance companies provide *certificates of insurance* (see Figure 7.3), which clearly note the types and amounts of coverage that the production company carries. A certificate is made out to the owner of each location and presented to him or her by the location manager prior to the production company's occupancy of the location. Most governments will not write a film permit until an insurance certificate is on file.

More sophisticated location owners, particularly large businesses and governments, will require that they be named "additional insured" and "loss payee" on the certificate. This enables them to make a claim directly to the insurance company and receive a check directly from the insurance company if a claim is paid, which protects them from a foot-dragging production company. The production company might have disappeared by the time the loss is discovered, and location owners will want to be sure they still have legal recourse to the party that will actually pay the bills—namely, the large, reputable insurance company that wrote the policy.

In order to obtain certificates of insurance, the location manager must provide the name and address of each location owner and the levels of coverage required to the producer or production manager, who then orders the certificates from the insurance company. Most insurance companies will process a certificate in a matter of hours and fax the document to the location owner, with an original copy following in the mail. The location manager should always keep a copy of each certificate in his or her files. These copies also come in handy if the scout or location manager needs to show owners of prospective locations that substantial coverage does exist.

CLEANUP

All productions, even small ones, can create quite a mess. When it comes to cleanup, there are several areas that will require attention. First, there is the amount of trash that is generated by a crew. This includes trash from the meals and snacks eaten on location—paper plates, cups, napkins, tablecloths,

ACORD. CERTIFICATE OF INSURANCE		DATE (MM/DD/YY) 3/31/94

PRODUCER

Admirable Insurance Co.
123 Bucks Drive
Accident, MD 21555

THIS CERTIFICATE IS ISSUED AS A MATTER OF INFORMATION ONLY AND CONFERS NO RIGHTS UPON THE CERTIFICATE HOLDER. THIS CERTIFICATE DOES NOT AMEND, EXTEND OR ALTER THE COVERAGE AFFORDED BY THE POLICIES BELOW.

COMPANIES AFFORDING COVERAGE

COMPANY A   XYZ Insurance

INSURED

Reckless Productions
456 Blue Sky Way
China Gove, NC 45678

COMPANY B   Old Faithful

COMPANY C

COMPANY D

COVERAGES

THIS IS TO CERTIFY THAT THE POLICIES OF INSURANCE LISTED BELOW HAVE BEEN ISSUED TO THE INSURED NAMED ABOVE FOR THE POLICY PERIOD INDICATED, NOTWITHSTANDING ANY REQUIREMENT, TERM OR CONDITION OF ANY CONTRACT OR OTHER DOCUMENT WITH RESPECT TO WHICH THIS CERTIFICATE MAY BE ISSUED OR MAY PERTAIN, THE INSURANCE AFFORDED BY THE POLICIES DESCRIBED HEREIN IS SUBJECT TO ALL THE TERMS, EXCLUSIONS AND CONDITIONS OF SUCH POLICIES. LIMITS SHOWN MAY HAVE BEEN REDUCED BY PAID CLAIMS.

CO LTR	TYPE OF INSURANCE	POLICY NUMBER	POLICY EFFECTIVE DATE (MM/DD/YY)	POLICY EXPIRATION DATE (MM/DD/YY)	LIMITS in thousands	
A	**GENERAL LIABILITY** X COMMERCIAL GENERAL LIABILITY ☐ CLAIMS MADE ☐ OCCUR X OWNER'S & CONTRACTOR'S PROT	C000567891	3/31/94	3/31/95	GENERAL AGGREGATE PRODUCTS - COMP/OP AGG PERSONAL & ADV INJURY EACH OCCURRENCE FIRE DAMAGE (Any one fire) MED EXP (Any one person)	$ 1,000 $ 1,000 $ 1,000 $ 500 $ 1,000 $ 1,000
A	**AUTOMOBILE LIABILITY** X ANY AUTO X ALL OWNED AUTOS ☐ SCHEDULED AUTOS X HIRED AUTOS X NON-OWNED AUTOS	B34567892	3/31/94	3/31/95	COMBINED SINGLE LIMIT BODILY INJURY (Per person) BODILY INJURY (Per accident) PROPERTY DAMAGE	$ 1,000 $ 1,000 $ 1,000 $ 500
A	**GARAGE LIABILITY** ☐ ANY AUTO				AUTO ONLY - EA ACCIDENT OTHER THAN AUTO ONLY: EACH ACCIDENT AGGREGATE	$ $ $
A	**EXCESS LIABILITY** X UMBRELLA FORM ☐ OTHER THAN UMBRELLA FORM	E987654320	3/31/94	3/31/95	EACH OCCURRENCE AGGREGATE	$ 1,000 $ 5,000 $
A	**WORKERS COMPENSATION AND EMPLOYERS' LIABILITY** THE PROPRIETOR/ PARTNERS/EXECUTIVE OFFICERS ARE: X INCL ☐ EXCL	WC12345678	3/31/94	3/31/95	STATUTORY LIMITS EACH ACCIDENT DISEASE - POLICY LIMIT DISEASE - EACH EMPLOYEE	$ 500 $ 500 $ 500
B	**OTHER** Misc Equipment Replacement Cost	A0000987654321	5/31/94	5/31/95	Limit $250,000 $1,500 deductible	

DESCRIPTION OF OPERATIONS/LOCATIONS/VEHICLES/SPECIAL ITEMS

Miscellaneous Equipment - Certificate Holder is insluded as Loss Payee for claims arising from negligence of Named insured

CERTIFICATE HOLDER

Anxious Equipment Rental
12345 South Blvd.
Orgone, Arkansas 09876

CANCELLATION

SHOULD ANY OF THE ABOVE DESCRIBED POLICIES BE CANCELLED BEFORE THE EXPIRATION DATE THEREOF, THE ISSUING COMPANY WILL ENDEAVOR TO MAIL 30 DAYS WRITTEN NOTICE TO THE CERTIFICATE HOLDER NAMED TO THE LEFT, BUT FAILURE TO MAIL SUCH NOTICE SHALL IMPOSE NO OBLIGATION OR LIABILITY OF ANY KIND UPON THE COMPANY, ITS AGENTS OR REPRESENTATIVES.

AUTHORIZED REPRESENTATIVE

ACORD 25-S (3/93)   © ACORD CORPORATION 1993

Figure 7.3 Certificate of insurance. [Copyright Accord, 1993; used with permission. Courtesy of Cohen Insurance, New York.]

food waste, cartons, packaging materials, and so on. Because all this material can be wet, messy, and smelly, a good stock of heavy-duty plastic lawn and leaf trash bags will be required. The work of the production crew also generates a surprising amount of trash. Blackout paper, plastic covers, lighting gels, adhesive tapes, used rope, drop cloths, and empty paint cans contribute greatly to the waste picture.

Crafts service is responsible for disposing of the trash and will have plenty of large plastic trash bags. Theoretically, it is responsible for cleanup, but more often than not, this responsibility will devolve onto the location department—because trash is the last thing anyone wants to think about and the location department is always the last to leave a site.

A substantial pile of trash bags, perhaps a dozen or more, can accumulate by the end of a shoot day. Generally, the amount is more than what the regular trash collectors will handle, particularly at a residence or small business, so the location department must find an alternative. Some cities, as a favor to the production industry, will arrange to have a special curbside trash pickup made within an hour of being called.

In smaller residential areas, ten or even twenty trash bags can be distributed among the neighbors, and a small gift or tip will buy their cooperation. A nearby business may allow the production to use its dumpster, especially if the owner is paid a bit of cash. Spending $20 or $30 in this way is much better than taking the time to haul the trash to a dump. Who wants to carry leaky trash bags in their car anyway?

For longer location occupancies (i.e., several days or weeks), it is wise to have a dumpster delivered to the location. A small- or medium-size one is inexpensive, holds a lot, and is trouble-free. Location managers should acquaint themselves with a reliable dumpster service and keep it on their contact list.

Unfortunately, dumpster services will not pick up trash that is dropped on the ground. The location department should therefore plan on picking up all the papers, cups, candy wrappers, and so on that were dropped by the production crew, both inside and outside the location. Having cigarette butt cans and trash bags strategically located by every door will make that job significantly easier, but the location department must be sure that all the litter has been picked up and all the trash bags removed. No one else will. Some areas of the country have strict recycling ordinances, so location managers need to be aware of how recyclables, mainly glass and aluminum containers, are handled locally.

DAMAGES

Damage to a location is closely related to general cleanup. As the location department is cleaning up, certain problems will become apparent. There may be obviously expensive damage, such as a shattered plate glass window or a broken chandelier, but such cases are rare.

The more common damage comes under the heading of excessive wear and tear. This can range from mud tracked on a rug to a scratch on a wood floor or a nick on a piece of furniture. Some things, like a scratch, cannot be repaired, and they are an unfortunate by-product of using a location. Hopefully, the location fee will be substantial enough to compensate owners for this sort of wear and tear. If owners are satisfied that they have been well paid and well treated, they will be inclined to overlook minor problems.

Sometimes, an additional fee is called for. Instead of the production company having an entire floor refinished at a cost of thousands of dollars, the owner may accept an extra $200 as compensation. If the location shows a lot of dirt and general disarray, the location manager should offer to hire a maid service to come in and do a thorough cleaning. That will satisfy 90 percent of the location owners and is a good bargain. The location manager should know several cleaning services that can be called in these situations. The bright side is that with all the moving of heavy furniture, many locations actually end up with a more thorough than usual cleaning anyway.

It is not uncommon for a location's lawns, shrubs, and gardens to suffer some trampling during a shoot. Because correcting this sort of damage requires expertise, tools, and supplies, the location manager should know some reliable landscape companies that can be called on short notice.

In any case where there has been slight damage or wear, it is always better for the location manager to settle the issue definitively before leaving the location. The easiest way is to offer more cash and let location owners handle all the details at their convenience. The location department does not want to have to worry about arranging for maid services or hiring someone to fix or replace tiny items—and then making sure the work is done to the owners' satisfaction. In terms of both time and effort on the part of the already harried location people, it is well worth the few extra dollars it may cost in the long run to let someone else handle such matters. Whether the location department handles damages or buys its way out, the most important thing is for owners to be left feeling that they have been treated fairly.

8

Types of Locations

INTERIOR VERSUS EXTERIOR LOCATIONS

There are big differences between an interior and an exterior location. In most sections of the country, bad weather is a major consideration, which will whimsically dictate whether an exterior shoot will be able to proceed as scheduled or not. Interior locations are almost never influenced by bad weather, which is why they are known as "cover sets." However, with exterior locations, when bad weather forces a change in the shooting day, all the detailed scheduling and preparation—police, support areas, parking, neighbors, and the like—must be redone.

Often, one support element may not be available on the new day—for example, a church basement that had been reserved on a Monday for an extras holding area might not be available on a Tuesday. This sort of problem might be enough to force an even more complex shoot change. Every change dictated by the weather or another unpredictable factor will have a domino effect on other arrangements at other locations, as the entire schedule is rearranged and refitted like a jigsaw puzzle.

With an exterior location, greater weight must be given to neighbors' reactions. Government and community cooperation is much more important to ensure a smooth shoot day. Additional security is required, and allowances must be made for all the disruptions to the shoot that will be caused by the public—as well as for all the disruptions to the neighborhood that will be caused by the crew.

An exterior location can be very large, sometimes extending hundreds of yards in every direction. All that the camera sees, and much more, must be controlled so that the filming can proceed smoothly. An interior location has the benefit of walls and a roof to shut out the prying and disruptive outside world.

Thus, shooting at an exterior location almost always requires more work than shooting at an interior one. To add insult to injury, normal production scheduling practice requires that all the exterior scenes be shot first, so all the location staff's most difficult work must be completed up front. The logic behind this is that the company can always retreat to the interior cover set in case of bad weather. Exteriors cannot be grouped toward the end of the shoot, nor can they be comfortably spaced, because of a simple question: If all the interiors have been shot and the weather is still bad, what can you shoot?

When all the cover sets have been used, there is no alternative except to rewrite the script or not shoot. A rewrite might be impossible, and not shooting but still paying the crew is financially disastrous for any production company. If bad weather will be a factor, production managers always insist that exteriors be scheduled first if at all possible. Because each scheduled day can easily cost $100,000 or more, they cannot take the risk of losing a day, no matter how hard it might be on any of the departments.

The bright side of this situation is that, given a run of good weather, the part of the production that is most difficult for the location team is over first. Once the exteriors have been shot, the location department's work becomes much more controllable. The completion of exterior shooting, then, should be a day of celebration for location people. Unfortunately, there are many unlucky productions in which exteriors are shot up to the last day due to weather and other schedule problems.

CONGESTED URBAN LOCATIONS

A densely populated, highly trafficked urban area is the most difficult type of exterior location. All the problems that occur with neighbors, government, and businesses come into play. No matter how much planning is done, it is almost impossible not to ruffle some feathers in an urban location. The best remedy is to get into and out of these sites as quickly as possible. But because urban shoots are unavoidable, location people should give careful consideration to the issues discussed here.

Urban locations present many problems for production support elements. Traffic and parking restrictions require that the honey wagons, dressing-room trailers, and motor homes be spread out along the curbs. This makes security more difficult, particularly with celebrities, because they are so close to a curious and usually intrusive public. Convenient extras holding areas and a crew meal area can be hard to find.

The best solution to these problems is to find a close hotel, church, private club, vacant storefront, or the like where some space can be rented by the day. Sometimes a deal can be made to buy out a portion of a parking lot where the transportation equipment can be staged, but that can get expensive as well as inconvenient, especially if a long walk to the location will be required. If there are many objections to parking the trucks on the street, then the production needs to be lucky enough to be near a cooperative hotel (i.e., one whose staff is not too uptight to mind members of the film crew running in and out all day), where several rooms can be rented.

A good location scout will be careful to find city locations that can accommodate the necessary support space required by a production. A beautiful location with no parking or rentable support space within fifteen city blocks is useless and will cause a great deal of frustration, trouble, and delay to all involved.

High-Rises

City high-rises in dense urban blocks involve a whole set of unique problems. Shooting on the twentieth or thirtieth floor of a building requires the use of elevators for everything. Elevators get full, and they get delayed. They often do not go to every floor, which means changing and more waiting. Freight elevators are usually needed to move equipment in and out. They may not be very large, and just one or two must serve hundreds of tenants. Therefore, they cannot be at the beck and call of the production company. It can take hours to load in and out using a high-rise freight elevator if other tenants need it too.

It can be impossible for production transportation units to park in a high-rise. Most high-rises have a basement loading dock that will accommodate just about any truck except a tractor-trailer. But because the space is extremely limited and many deliveries are expected during the day, most high-rises place severe restrictions on the unload-load times during business hours.

Finding enough electric power to operate production lighting equipment can be difficult in a high-rise because breaker boxes are few and far between. Operating a generator is out of the question on any but the lowest floors because of the long cable runs involved.

In some buildings, the tenants might have no patience with the disruption caused by a production crew. They pay high rents for peace, quiet, and accessibility and do not want any of those things interfered with.

Finding support areas in a high-rise can be difficult because most of these buildings are filled with working offices and do not have an inch to spare. Therefore, corridors quickly get clogged with equipment, which then becomes a safety concern to the building's tenants, who may complain loudly. Dressing areas and holding areas are hard to find because space is so tight. And again, getting anywhere in a high-rise via elevator can take a surprisingly long time.

More and more high-rises are incorporating hotels with meeting and guest rooms into their design. These buildings can be the perfect answer to a production's support needs because at least they have space that can be rented. They are the exception, though.

Ultimately, shooting in an urban high-rise requires a much leaner production style and is often prohibitively difficult for anything but the simplest shoot. Sometimes, more accessible suburban sites should be sought first. Shooting in a high-rise on weekends and holidays is much, much simpler and must be seriously considered for more demanding shoots that absolutely must have a high-rise office for its spectacular view or other attributes.

Road Closings and Detours

When productions involve car-chase scenes, sidewalk scenes, or any other sort of "urban activity" requiring multiple camera setups, actors, and background action, then the traffic on those locations must be controlled, which demands a significant amount of preplanning. The location manager must coordinate all the aspects of a road closure with the affected public, commercial enterprises, and government agencies. This includes businesses, residents, the police department, the local transit and traffic department, and someone from a government agency (most likely the film commission) that has executive authority over the use of government or public property.

The passport to accomplishing all this coordination and getting the shot is the film permit—a misnomer because it can be used for video productions, still-photo shoots, and even live theatrical events. Film permits are discussed in greater detail in a later section of this chapter.

Most local governments are willing to close a portion of a road for a short period, provided the production company has notified the persons affected by the closure and not found any objections. Because roads can be either town, county, state, or federally owned, the location manager must find out who is actually responsible for the affected stretch of road. The local police will help determine the jurisdiction and direct the location manager to the proper authority.

There are standard procedures for closing roads, sidewalks, and alleys. Construction companies constantly need to close thoroughfares, so most governments have created special permits for that purpose. Basically, production companies use those same permits, except they are called "film permits" if the jurisdiction is sophisticated enough to have them. The permit specifies the date and duration of the closure and the details of who will have authority over the closure.

If a road is to be closed for more than a day or two, most governments require that the general public be given substantial advance notice of the closure. This usually consists of a large sign at the beginning of the detour noting that on a certain date between specific hours, the road will be closed and a marked detour route will be created. The marked detour route consists of obvious direction signs at each intersection, which will lead motorists around the affected area and back to the unblocked portion of the road.

The public is familiar with such signs primarily because of their use when major road or bridge work requires a road closure. The advance notice warns people to practice the detour route and be sure they have no special requirements (e.g., furniture or construction deliveries) that would absolutely necessitate their using the road at that time.

Most road closure permits for production require that delivery trucks be allowed to get through with minimal delay. Emergency vehicles must be able to get through with little or no delay. Prior to granting the permit, the local authorities will require that the production company contact all the directly affected businesses and residents to inform them of the detour and make sure they have no strong objections. Obtaining this permission in advance is important to the production company as well because it does not want last-minute trouble or delays created by irate neighbors.

COUNTRY ROADS

Many productions call for scenic country roads. Nearly every car commercial and many still-photo ads require beautiful driving shots. In feature films and TV movies, writers and directors require scene after scene of dialogue while driving. Location people should count on the fact that every contemporary dramatic script will need at least a handful of different road locations.

Roads are judged mainly on three quite different but nonetheless important qualities: the look, the amount of traffic they support, and the smoothness of their surface.

The Look

First of all, the road must have the look described in the script. If it is supposed to be a desolate country road, it must have no buildings or other structures that would give it an urban feel, including high-rises on the horizon. Location roads for period film productions require even more careful attention. They must be free of any homes, signs, lights, power lines, shops, and so on that are not correct for the period.

Finding a road that has an appropriate period look can be a special challenge. For example, if a 1950s look is needed, then homes, gas stations, and street lights must be from that period. It is nearly impossible for an art department to completely dress a road to create the proper period look, so the location department must do its best to find something that needs as little dressing as possible. Discovering a suitable stretch of road takes a bit of imagination and familiarity with some of the art department's tricks.

Searching for a scenic road can be one of the most relaxing and fun location scouting jobs. It simply requires a good visual sense, a good map, and a good radio to help pass the time while driving through the countryside. The best leads for beautiful roads are local road commission workers. Everyone has a handful of his or her favorite scenic routes, and tourist offices as well as road commissions may already have the area's most scenic routes mapped out. If a topographic map is available, then preference should be given to roads that run through valleys. They are usually among the most scenic because the distant ridges make an attractive backdrop and provide a nice perspective to any shot.

Amount of Traffic

Given the amount of production equipment required for most road shots, the volume of traffic on any given road is very important. A production will need to close the section of road on which it is working, so easily navigated detours must be available for drivers whose normal route will be blocked.

Detailed maps of an area must be consulted to determine how difficult it will be to set up a detour. Except in the most rural areas, detours are usually easy enough to create and only affect those persons who do not have access to their homes or businesses as quickly as they normally would. If a detour only lasts a day or two, the inconvenience will be over before anyone actually realizes its cause or thinks to take action against it.

For those individuals who live or work along the blocked portion of the road and whose normal access is denied, special care must be taken to ensure that they are able to come and go as they please. These people must be warned well in advance of any road closure and told that they will be given special escorts into and out of the area. Arrangements also need to be made for any sort of delivery, school buses, trash pickup, home service providers, and mass transit. People enjoy special treatment, and if treated with concern, friendliness, and respect, they will respond favorably.

Smoothness of the Surface

Shooting film or video from a moving vehicle is a tricky affair. It requires special "camera-car" vehicles and camera mounts. Many times, the vehicle being shot is towed on a "process trailer," but the illusion is that it is being driven. In order for this illusion to be created effectively, the vehicles must be traveling at a normal rate of speed. This requires a very smooth road surface, without joints, bumps, or potholes.

Even small bumps on any sort of road surface will jolt the camera. Bumps that would hardly be noticed in normal driving situations are magnified tremendously by the camera and lens and will look like an earthquake when projected. The availability of good, smooth roads is not such a problem in Sunbelt states, where the lack of deep freezes minimizes the buckling and potholes typical of roads in colder climates. Finding a "perfectly smooth" road can be quite difficult. The best approach is for the location department to search diligently and get some tips from the local highway department about where to find the most recently surfaced roads.

FILM PERMITS

Film permits (see Figure 8.1) usually are required only in cities that have experienced a significant amount of location production requiring the cooperation of the local government. They are an outgrowth of the need to spell out the rules that a production company must follow when using public property and interfering with the activities that normally occur on that property. Areas that encourage productions make permits easy and inexpensive to obtain. Areas that are overloaded with productions may make them harder and more expensive to obtain.

A permit will usually contain at least the following information:

- Name of the production and the production company
- Date and location of the shoot
- Exact time period during which filming will occur (e.g., 6:00 A.M. to 9:00 P.M.)
- Exact area of the shooting (e.g., Calvert Street between 22d and 23d Streets)
- Size of crew and number of production vehicles allowed

```
            APPLICATION FOR PERMISSION TO FILM            1
                  Metropolitan Dade County, Florida       PERMIT NO.

                                    Date Initiated  03/19/93

Name of Applicant _____  Title _____
Firm _____
Address _____  Phone  (123) 555-9876
        _____  Fax  _____

Local Contact Information: The Permittee shall have on site a responsible representative empowered
with authority over the filming director, filming crews, participants and filming operation.

Name _____  Title _____
Address _____  Phone  _____
        _____  Fax  _____

Type of Production  Features              Product/Service  _____

  If motion picture, submit script.  Title  _____

No. Locally Employed    Amount to be spent within Dade County ____  $0.00
Cast _____ Crew _____  Production days in Dade County _____

Insurance Company Name  _____
Policy Number  _____
Coverage Amount  _____  Expiration Date  01/01/02
```

Location/Personnel/Equipment	Start Date	End Date	Days/Time	Approval	Charges*
Key Biscayne	01/02/93	01/11/93			$100.00

```
  *Parking Fees Apply              Estimated Total Charges    $100.00

Description of scene(s) for which the requested County facilities, personnel and/or equipment will
be used. (Include approximate number of people involved, special equipment, and other relevant
information.)
```

PLEASE SUBMIT A COPY OF THIS PERMIT TO FACILITY UPON ARRIVAL.

The permittee shall agree to assume all risk in the use of County property in the permitted operation and shall be solely
responsible and answerable in damages for all accidents and injury to person or property and shall be covenant and agree
to indemnify and keep harmless the County and its officers and employees from any and all claims, suits, losses, damages,
or injury to person or property.

```
_____      _____    _____
Name of Company                    Signature of Authorized Representative   Date

                             RV    _____    _____
                                   Approved, Film Coordinator          Date
```

Permittee shall keep a copy of this approved permit and
attachments on location while filming on Dade County
property. For further information and assistance, contact:

OFFICE OF FILM AND TELEVISION COORDINATION
PARK & RECREATION DEPARTMENT
50 S.W. 32nd Road, Miami, Florida 33129
Phone: (305)372-3456, Fax: (305)579-2509

Figure 8.1 Typical film permit generated by a word processor.
[Courtesy of the Miami Office of Film and Television Coordination.]

- Description of the action to be shot
- Any requirement to close sidewalks or streets

Prior to a permit's being granted, the production company must present its request to the local authorities at a production meeting. The presentation must include all the above information, in writing and with clear diagrams.

The general rule in traffic control is that the local traffic department—which has frontline authority over roads, sidewalks, and alleys—must determine whether the closing of a particular route will cause injury, harm, or loss to the public that depends on those thoroughfares to be open. This is usually not a big problem unless the request involves closing a busy street at rush hour. In most areas, detours can easily be set up. Although it can be inconvenient, the public is accustomed to encountering closed sidewalks or taking short detours due to construction or repair projects. A detour or slowdown due to a production is a novelty, and some short-term inconvenience can be tolerated, provided emergency vehicles always have access.

Of course, production companies can abuse road closures in many ways. They might shut down more of an area than originally discussed, or they might run late, creating a gross inconvenience for residents or drivers. Local authorities are wary of this potential for abuse because such abuses can prompt vocal complaints from angry taxpaying citizens who do not appreciate the annoyance. The permit system is designed to avoid this situation by enabling the government and the production company to reach a mutual understanding regarding the authorized limits of the work so that it can proceed with minimal inconvenience to all concerned.

The police department also plays an integral role in the process. It legally enforces the terms of the permit. The police are usually the only people who can legally direct traffic around or away from the shooting area. The traffic department might make all the arrangements, but on-site, the police control the operation. It is important for the crew to have a good relationship with the police because police officers have the authority to make immediate decisions regarding public safety no matter what the permit might say. If police officers feel good about the production, they will be more flexible. If not, they can be a real hindrance to getting the shots. Ultimately, if the police are kept informed and treated as an important part of the production, they will be much more cooperative.

Municipal traffic departments will be conservative at a production meeting, not wanting to grant as much as the production company might want or need. Once the production is on-site, though, if the police determine that it is safe at a given moment to grant the production company's requests, then they have the power to do so. This can be helpful when a director decides that he or she needs more of the street blocked in order to get a shot.

There are two methods for dealing with urban traffic conditions. The first is to completely shut down a street so that neither vehicles nor pedestrians can have access to the shooting area. This is most convenient for the production company because it then has full control of the shot and its backgrounds and can proceed with minimal distractions. It requires barricading the street, marking detours, and having police direct traffic at each barricade.

The second approach is to allow traffic to flow through the site except when there is a camera rehearsal or an actual take. In this situation, police are stationed at the edge of the set and are cued to stop traffic or allow it to proceed according to commands from the assistant director. This creates an awkward, slow-moving situation because the shooting crew must wait for the backgrounds to clear before rolling the camera. It also can be dangerous to have traffic flowing through a set where crew members are likely to be paying more attention to their work than to the dangers of stepping out in front of a moving car.

Most assistant directors want every exterior city location "locked up and shut down" so that the shoot can proceed uninterrupted. Although this is the ideal situation in terms of both safety and efficiency, sometimes it cannot be accomplished because of the disruption it causes to local traffic. The locals see that the camera rolls for only ten minutes an hour. From their point of view, it is therefore better to stop traffic for only ten minutes an hour, thereby inconveniencing far fewer residents, commuters, and potential customers.

The solution must be determined on a case-by-case basis, according to the characteristics of each location. Again, although it is ideal to shut down a street, that is often impractical, unnecessary, or simply impossible (e.g., closing a major commuter artery at rush hour). Controlling traffic through walkie-talkies is usually the realistic compromise, in which everyone loses a little time but nothing comes to a dead halt and an acceptable level of safety is maintained.

INTERNATIONAL LOCATIONS

The United States is the uncontested production capital of the world, but there are still plenty of opportunities for location shooting in other countries. Although only the largest productions will actually send a U.S. location manager abroad, the production manager or producer must be aware of certain location issues in order to see that a shoot outside the United States goes smoothly.

The easiest solution is to find a local person or company in the area of the country where the shooting will occur and hire that individual or firm as the local contact or "fixer." Ideally, the contact will be able to handle most of the location manager's responsibilities. It is not possible to find a person versed in production everywhere in the world, just as it is not possible to find one in every corner of the United States. However, finding someone from the local radio station or newspaper to serve as a guide/contact/fixer is usually a good bet. Such a person is likely to understand the demands of production best.

The topic of international location production would require a book of its own, because every country is different. However, the following checklist should help any producer or photographer get started and avoid the most formidable problems:

- The U.S. production company should find a local contact, photographer, production company, or television station and hire that person or firm (or someone recommended by that person or firm) to be the location contact/scout/manager. Many countries have film commissions that can help a production company find such individuals or firms. The tourist office will be happy to help.

- The country's immigration policies must be investigated to be sure that members of the production company will be allowed to work there. (The company must remember to indicate that its workers are being *paid* in the United States by a U.S. firm.) Special visas may be required. The country's embassy in Washington, D.C., can provide this information.
- Restrictions imposed by the United States and the foreign country on the importation/exportation of equipment must be investigated. Some countries charge excessive duty on imported production equipment; some completely forbid its importation; and most allow it to be imported duty-free with the proper paperwork, usually an AIT Carnet. Again, the particular country's embassy in Washington, D.C., can provide this information. The nearest office of the U.S. Customs Service can advise the production company of the rules and regulations regarding taking equipment out of the United States and bringing it back in again.
- A good travel agent experienced in international business travel should handle all reservations for planes, cars, and hotels.
- The production company's insurance agent should be contacted regarding restrictions on insurance coverage in foreign countries.
- Differences in electric power frequency, voltage, and outlet plug types; television systems (PAL, NTSC); and automobile driving rules must all be checked out.
- Members of the production company who will be going abroad should inform their doctor of where they will be traveling and ask for advice on what immunizations to obtain before departing and what medications to carry with them.

- Individuals who will be working abroad should purchase a travel guide to the country and read it from cover to cover—as soon as possible.

This is not a terribly daunting list, but then again, what the members of a production company will need depends on where they will be going. Each foreign country is different. Working abroad presents new bureaucratic challenges that are not normally faced by people in the United States. These challenges can be surprising, and it would be best for novices not to take on too much responsibility in the international arena until they have gained some real experience.

State Film Commissions

Note: Film commission phone numbers are subject to change. Therefore, if any of the numbers below is incorrect, try directory assistance for the state's capitol and ask for the number of that state's department of tourism information and/or the department of economic development (i.e., marketing). The film commission is generally a division of the economic development or tourism office.

Alabama	(800) 633-5898	California	(213) 736-2465
			Fax: (213) 736-3159
Alaska	(907) 562-4163		
	Fax: (907) 563-3575	Colorado	(303) 866-2778
			Fax: (303) 866-2251
Arizona	(800) 528-8421		
	(602) 542-5011	Connecticut	(203) 258-4301
Arkansas	(501) 682-7676	Delaware	(302) 736-4271

Florida	(904) 487-1100	Montana	(406) 444-2654
	Fax: (904) 487-3014		
		Nebraska	(800) 426-6505
Georgia	(404) 656-3591		(402) 471-2593
	(404) 656-3544		
		Nevada	(702) 486-7150
Hawaii	(808) 548-4535		
	(808) 548-3006	New Hampshire	(603) 271-2598
Idaho	(800) 942-8338	New Jersey	(201) 648-6279
	(208) 334-2470		
	Fax: (208) 334-2631	New Mexico	(800) 545-9871
			(505) 827-8580
Illinois	(312) 814-3600		Fax: (505) 827-4047
Indiana	(317) 232-8829	New York	(212) 575-6570
			Fax: (212) 840-7149
Iowa	(515) 281-5522		
		North Carolina	(919) 733-9900
Kansas	(913) 296-4927		
		North Dakota	(800) 437-2077
Kentucky	(502) 564-3456		(701) 224-2810
Louisiana	(504) 342-8150	Ohio	(800) 848-1300
			(614) 466-2284
Maine	(207) 289-5710		
	(207) 289-5705	Oklahoma	(405) 843-9770
Maryland	(301) 333-6633	Oregon	(800) 547-7842
			(503) 373-1232
Massachusetts	(617) 973-8800		Fax: (503) 581-5115
Michigan	(313) 256-2000	Pennsylvania	(717) 787-5333
	(313) 379-0642		
		Rhode Island	(401) 277-3456
Minnesota	(612) 332-6493		
		South Carolina	(803) 737-0400
Mississippi	(601) 359-3449		
	Fax: (601) 359-2832	South Dakota	(605) 773-3301
Missouri	(314) 751-9050	Tennessee	(800) 251-8594
	(314) 751-4241		(615) 741-3456

Texas	(512) 469-9111	Washington	(206) 464-7148
	Fax: (512) 473-2312	State	Fax: (206) 464-7222

U.S. Virgin Islands	(809) 774-8784	West Virginia	(800) 225-5982
	(809) 775-1444		(304) 348-2286

Utah	(800) 453-8824	Wisconsin	(608) 267-3456

Vermont	(802) 828-3236	Wyoming	(800) 458-6657
	Fax: (802) 828-3233		(307) 777-7777

Virginia	(804) 371-8204

Washington, D.C.	(202) 727-6600

Appendix B

Getting a Job in the Location Department

Location scouting is one of the few areas in media production where lots of experience is *not* necessary to get a foot in the door or land a first job. Because scouting requires more talent in the areas of good taste and common sense, and less in the area of complicated technical skills, a true greenhorn can progress quickly through the ranks.

It is almost impossible to get a paying job in any area of film, television, or photography with just a formal education (i.e., college or technical school). Production companies want people with real-life work experience in every job. This is a difficult concept for people who have sweated their way through four or more years of college and spent $100,000 or more to obtain a degree. They will want to jump right in and start making the big bucks. Unfortunately, it doesn't work that way.

My advice to everyone having a hard time finding his or her first job in production is to volunteer or do an "unpaid internship" with a production company. Consider a six-month internship to be a part of your educational expense. After spending sixteen years going to school, unpaid, what's another six months, particularly when it is the icing on the cake? Even after six months, you may not have a full-time job, but you will have made enough all-important connections to progress in your career if you have impressed the right people with hard work, attention to detail, and a cheerful attitude—which, by the way, are the top three attributes of a good location person.

This book goes into great detail about the technical skills and general knowledge of production that a location manager should have. It may take several years of steady work to become a truly competent location manager who is trusted enough to work on the big features and TV commercials. But virtually anyone can tack on the title of "location scout" and go to work. Although there is some finesse involved, it does not take the brain of a rocket scientist to "go find a nice-looking living room." Chances are, between friends and relatives, you will come up with several good choices without having to knock on a single stranger's door. And your friends and relatives will love you for the opportunity to get into the movies, not to mention the location fee.

Even if location scouting or management is not your ultimate career goal, scouting is still a good place to start for any area of the business, unless you are a die-hard sound, light, or camera techie. And even if you are, a little location department experience will help you become a more sympathetic team player.

Scouting is an almost foolproof entry-level job. If you are honest, have done a little studying, and are pleasantly determined, and if you have good taste and common sense as well, you cannot be a bad location scout. Remember, your work will always be double- and triple-checked by more experienced people, so any errors will be caught and corrected by a sympathetic superior. Your work will generally be completed before any big money is spent on shooting, so your errors will not cost anyone money. This cannot be said about the majority of media jobs, in which most errors cause serious trouble and hard feelings and cost a lot of money.

The easiest way to start is to identify the largest production companies in your area and let them know that you are interested in and available for scouting assignments, on a free intern basis. Tell them that if you don't find the location they are looking for, you don't want to be paid. Any producer will be delighted to pay a fair finder's fee for a good location. After you have established a track record, you will likely graduate to a day rate.

In the meantime, it is helpful to assemble a list of the more commonly used location possibilities—like homes, business offices, stores, and good roads—from friends, family, and acquaintances. Having "preapproved" locations will impress producers and enable you to make money with less work. At worst, you can deduct your expenses for car mileage, still film, cameras, meals on the road, and so forth from your gross taxable income.

As a scout, you will generally have direct access to the key creatives and administrators on a production. You will not be a faceless gofer stationed by the photocopier for eighteen hours a day. At the right moment, you can let the right person know that you don't want to be a scout all your life. Instead, you want to learn more about _____. If you have done a good job as a scout, earning trust and respect from the production team, you will find many more open doors.

Finally, the location department is a good place to soak up the real-life details of a production—to learn firsthand what a Louma crane does, what a honey wagon is, and how an AD runs the often near chaos of a shooting set. It is a priceless education. Best of luck!

Index